# SolarWinds Server & Application Monitor: Deployment and Administration

An intuitive guide to implementing and calibrating SolarWinds Server & Application Monitor with minimum hassle

**Justin M. Brant**

PUBLISHING

BIRMINGHAM - MUMBAI

# SolarWinds Server & Application Monitor: Deployment and Administration

First published: November 2013

Production Reference: 1131113

Published by Packt Publishing Ltd.
Livery Place
35 Livery Street
Birmingham B3 2PB, UK.

ISBN 978-1-78328-245-6

www.packtpub.com

Cover Image by Aniket Sawant (aniket_sawant_photography@hotmail.com)

# Credits

**Author**
Justin M. Brant

**Reviewers**
Sam Namiq
Jeremy D. Phillips

**Acquisition Editors**
Vinay Argekar
Edward Gordon

**Commissioning Editors**
Neil Alexander
Subho Gupta

**Technical Editors**
Amit Shetty
Rohit Kumar Singh

**Project Coordinator**
Joel Goveya

**Proofreader**
Lawrence A. Herman

**Indexer**
Hemangini Bari

**Production Coordinator**
Shantanu Zagade

**Cover Work**
Shantanu Zagade

# About the Author

**Justin M. Brant** has over 15 years of IT industry experience. As an adolescent, he was mentored by his grandfather Edgar J. Reynolds, a retired Naval Oceans Systems Center (NOSC) Electronic Engineer, who trained him on systems such as Apple II, Macintosh Plus, and Windows 2.x.

His grandfather's guidance led to a position at Datel Systems, where he began his career in the IT industry. Shortly thereafter, Justin and his brother Gregory created Blue Sun Design LLC, a consulting group focused on the Information Technology Infrastructure Library (ITIL) Framework, designed to support small to medium-sized business networks. He later joined the Biomedical Research Institute of America Institutional Review Board (BioMed IRB) as the Network Administrator, where he maintained the IT infrastructure consistent with FDA regulations for electronic records and patient confidentiality.

Presently, Justin is the Technical Support Manager at Integrated Default Solutions (IDSolutions), where he manages a team of five help desk technicians supporting 1,300 enterprise users nationwide. His position is multifaceted, involving network support, strategy, design, transition, and operation. His primary responsibilities include refining processes and security measures through developing and maintaining the IDSolutions Standard Operating Procedure (SOP) manual. In addition, he is the in-house specialist for the ShoreTel PBX & ECC VoIP system.

I would like to dedicate this book to my grandfather, Edgar J. Reynolds, for being ahead of his time and sparking my interest in technology. I would like to thank Fred Fox and Gary Shkedy, Executive Directors at BioMed IRB, who were pivotal mentors regarding IT health care security regulations; also, David Brassfield, Amelia Cline, Jeremy Phillips, Petersan Jean-Pierre, Troy Muncy, Sam Namiq, and Syneca Horton, for supporting this project as technical reviewers and advisors, and my mother Vicki Aznoe, for encouraging me to continuously write. In addition, I would like to thank the Packt Publishing team for their excellent ongoing communication and constructive feedback.

# About the Reviewers

**Sam Namiq** is a highly motivated and knowledgeable technology professional skilled at administering complex computer systems running in Windows environments. He holds many industry certifications, such as CCNA, MCP, MCTS, MCITP 2008:EA, and MCSA 2012. He has over 15 years of experience working in the IT field. He has experience in designing, deploying, and administering Active Directory (2003, 2008, 2008R2, and 2012), deploying and managing Symantec Endpoint Protection, deploying and administering Dell AppAssure, and deploying and administering Exchange Servers (2003, 2007, 2010, and 2013). In addition, he has experience in deploying and configuring SolarWinds Network Performance Monitor (NPM), Virtualization using ESXi and Hyper-V, Cisco routers and switches, and many other IT solutions.

**Jeremy D. Phillips** works as a software programmer/developer in San Diego, CA. He has been writing code since the early 90s starting with DOS on monochrome screens in grade school, and has an interest in reverse engineering and software security.

> I'd like to thank my family for providing consistent support in my endeavors.

# www.PacktPub.com

## Support files, eBooks, discount offers and more

You might want to visit www.PacktPub.com for support files and downloads related to your book.

Did you know that Packt offers eBook versions of every book published, with PDF and ePub files available? You can upgrade to the eBook version at www.PacktPub.com and as a print book customer, you are entitled to a discount on the eBook copy. Get in touch with us at service@packtpub.com for more details.

At www.PacktPub.com, you can also read a collection of free technical articles, sign up for a range of free newsletters and receive exclusive discounts and offers on Packt books and eBooks.

http://PacktLib.PacktPub.com

Do you need instant solutions to your IT questions? PacktLib is Packt's online digital book library. Here, you can access, read and search across Packt's entire library of books.

## Why Subscribe?

- Fully searchable across every book published by Packt
- Copy and paste, print and bookmark content
- On demand and accessible via web browser

## Free Access for Packt account holders

If you have an account with Packt at www.PacktPub.com, you can use this to access PacktLib today and view nine entirely free books. Simply use your login credentials for immediate access.

# Table of Contents

# Preface

SolarWinds Server & Application Monitor (SAM) is a comprehensive network-monitoring service that provides a variety of tools designed to prevent downtime and quickly pinpoint network-related issues. SolarWinds SAM is suitable for organizations of all sizes, ranging from small businesses to large enterprises.

The chief responsibility of a network or systems administrator is to ensure high availability of IT services. Therefore, it is vital to have around-the-clock network surveillance and to be alerted when issues arise. Deploying SolarWinds SAM will help accomplish this and ensure that service-level agreements are met.

The product can be hosted on a server with specifications as low as a single core 2.4 GHz CPU, with 4 GB RAM and 4 GB free hard disk space. These minimum requirements may not suffice for larger networks, although the application rarely needs to be hosted on a "high-end" dedicated server. Supported operating systems include Windows Server 2003, Windows Server 2008 R2, and Windows Server 2012, running in 32-bit mode. Procedures throughout this book are applicable to Windows Server 2008 R2 and will translate well to the other supported versions.

This book will provide a practical overview of SolarWinds SAM, and include tutorials on how to systematically and expeditiously begin monitoring your entire network. It will explain how to deploy the product and tailor it for your environment, with an emphasis on best practices concerning bandwidth and security implications. After completing this book, you will have sufficient hands-on experience to thoroughly monitor all servers, applications, and network devices encompassed within your organization.

# What this book covers

*Chapter 1, Deployment Strategy,* prepares administrators for deploying SolarWinds SAM by providing tutorials on configuring monitoring services and protocols on servers, common network devices, and VMHosts.

*Chapter 2, Installing and Configuring SolarWinds SAM,* serves as a quick installation and Network Sonar Wizard walkthrough for deploying SolarWinds SAM.

*Chapter 3, Customizing SolarWinds SAM,* provides tutorials for adding, managing, and classifying nodes. Groups and dependencies are also covered, followed by procedures on how to back up all the customizations.

*Chapter 4, Events, Traps, and Alerts,* contains examples and procedures on how to enable, configure, and manage events, SNMP traps, and alerts.

*Chapter 5, Syslog, Reporting, and Network Atlas,* consists of an overview of how to decipherer and utilize the Syslog, run reports, and includes a tutorial on how to design a network map via the Orion Network Atlas utility.

*Appendix, Troubleshooting,* includes troubleshooting tips on some common network monitoring service and SolarWinds SAM issues.

# What you need for this book

Before you get started, you will need to have the SolarWinds SAM physical media on hand, or have previously downloaded the fully functional 30-day trial from:

```
http://www.solarwinds.com/server-application-monitor.aspx
```

A machine running Windows Server 2003, Windows Server 2008 R2, or Windows Server 2012 should be available for installing the product.

# Who this book is for

This book is intended for network and systems administrators new to network-monitoring services and/or SolarWinds SAM.

# Conventions

In this book, you will find a number of styles of text that distinguish between different kinds of information. Here are some examples of these styles, and an explanation of their meaning.

Code words in text are shown as follows: "We can include other contexts through the use of the `include` directive."

Any command-line input or output is written as follows:

```
C:\>telnet 192.168.1.230
```

**New terms** and **important words** are shown in bold. Words that you see on the screen, in menus or dialog boxes for example, appear in the text like this: "Click on the **Add** button."

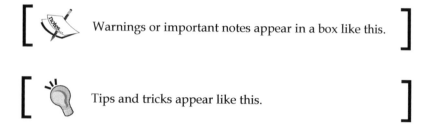

Warnings or important notes appear in a box like this.

Tips and tricks appear like this.

# Reader feedback

Feedback from our readers is always welcome. Let us know what you think about this book—what you liked or may have disliked. Reader feedback is important for us to develop titles that you really get the most out of.

To send us general feedback, simply send an e-mail to feedback@packtpub.com, and mention the book title via the subject of your message.

If there is a topic that you have expertise in and you are interested in either writing or contributing to a book, see our author guide on www.packtpub.com/authors.

# Customer support

Now that you are the proud owner of a Packt book, we have a number of things to help you to get the most from your purchase.

# Errata

Although we have taken every care to ensure the accuracy of our content, mistakes do happen. If you find a mistake in one of our books—maybe a mistake in the text or the code—we would be grateful if you would report this to us. By doing so, you can save other readers from frustration and help us improve subsequent versions of this book. If you find any errata, please report them by visiting http://www.packtpub.com/submit-errata, selecting your book, clicking on the **errata submission form** link, and entering the details of your errata. Once your errata are verified, your submission will be accepted and the errata will be uploaded on our website, or added to any list of existing errata, under the Errata section of that title. Any existing errata can be viewed by selecting your title from http://www.packtpub.com/support.

# Piracy

Piracy of copyright material on the Internet is an ongoing problem across all media. At Packt, we take the protection of our copyright and licenses very seriously. If you come across any illegal copies of our works, in any form, on the Internet, please provide us with the location address or website name immediately so that we can pursue a remedy.

Please contact us at copyright@packtpub.com with a link to the suspected pirated material.

We appreciate your help in protecting our authors, and our ability to bring you valuable content.

# Questions

You can contact us at questions@packtpub.com if you are having a problem with any aspect of the book, and we will do our best to address it.

# 1
# Deployment Strategy

A deployment strategy is the most comprehensive approach before introducing a network monitoring service to your environment. The deployment strategy for SolarWinds **Server & Application Monitor (SAM)** should identify what should be monitored, then prepare servers, devices, and applications (nodes) to be imported into SolarWinds SAM.

Procedures in this chapter are not required pre-deployment, as it is possible after deployment to populate SolarWinds SAM with nodes; however, it is recommended. Even after deployment, you should still enable and configure advanced monitoring services on your vital nodes.

SolarWinds SAM uses three types of protocols to poll management data:

- **Simple Network Management Protocol (SNMP)**: This is the most common network management service protocol. To utilize it, SNMP must be enabled and an SNMP community string must be assigned on the server, device, or application. The community string is essentially a password that is sent between a node and SolarWinds SAM. Once the community string is set and assigned, the node is permitted to expose management data to SolarWinds SAM, in the form of variables. Currently, there are three versions of SNMP: v1, v2c, and v3.

SolarWinds SAM uses SNMPv2c by default. To poll using SNMPv1, you must disable SNMPv2c on the device. Similarly, to poll using SNMPv3, you must configure your devices and SolarWinds SAM accordingly. We will be using SNMPv2c in all procedures referenced in this book.

- **Windows Management Instrumentation (WMI)**: This has added functionality by incorporating Windows specific communications and security features. WMI comes preinstalled on Windows by default but is not automatically enabled and configured. WMI is not exclusive to Windows server platforms; it comes installed on all modern Microsoft operating systems, and can also be used to poll desktop operating systems, such as Windows 7.

- **Internet Control Message Protocol (ICMP)**: This is the most basic of the three; it simply sends echo requests (pings) to a server or device for status, response time, and packet loss. SolarWinds SAM uses ICMP in conjunction with SNMP and WMI. Nodes can be configured to poll with ICMP exclusively, but you miss out on CPU, memory, and volume data. Some devices can only be polled with ICMP, although in most instances you will rarely use ICMP exclusively.

**Trying to decide between SNMP and WMI?**

SNMP is more standardized and provides data that you may not be able to poll with WMI, such as interface information. In addition, polling a single WMI-enabled node uses roughly five times the resources required to poll the same node with SNMP.

This chapter will explain how to prepare for SolarWinds SAM deployment, by enabling and configuring network management services and protocols on:

- Windows servers
- VMware hosts
- Common network devices

In this chapter and throughout the book we will reference service accounts. A service account is an account created to handoff credentials to SolarWinds SAM. Service accounts are a best practice primarily for security reasons, but also to ensure that user accounts do not become locked out.

# Enabling and configuring SNMP on Windows

Procedures listed in this section will explain how to enable SNMP and then assign a community string, on Windows Server 2008 R2.

 All Windows server-related procedures in this book are performed on Windows Server 2008 R2. Procedures vary slightly in other supported versions.

## Installing an SNMP service on Windows

This procedure explains how to install the SNMP service on Windows Server 2008 R2.

1. Log in to a Windows server.

2. Navigate to **Start Menu** | **Control Panel** | **Administrative Tools** | **Server Manager**.

 In order to see **Administrative Tools** in the **Control Panel**, you may need to select **View by: Small Icons** or **Large Icons**.

3. Select **Features** and click on **Add Features**.

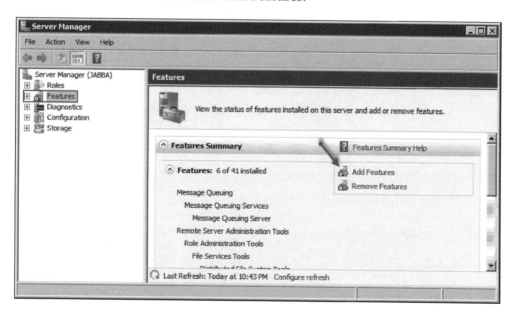

4.   Check **SNMP Services**, then click on **Next** and **Install**.

5.   Click on **Close**.

# Assigning an SNMP community string on Windows

This procedure explains how to assign a community string on Windows 2008 R2, and ensure that the SNMP service is configured to run automatically on start up.

1.   Log in to a Windows server.

2.   Navigate to **Start Menu | Control Panel | Administrative Tools | Services**.

3.   Double-click on **SNMP Service**.

4.   On the **General** tab, select **Automatic** under **Startup type**.

5.   Select the **Agent** tab and ensure **Physical, Applications, Internet,** and **End-to-end** are all checked under the **Service** area.

6.   Optionally, enter a **Contact** person and system **Location**.

7.   Select the **Security** tab and click on the **Add** button under **Accepted community names**.

8.   Enter a **Community Name** and click on the **Add** button. For example, we used S4MS3rv3r. We recommend using something secure, as this is a password.

Community String and **Community Name** mean the same thing.

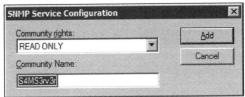

**READ ONLY** community rights will normally suffice. A detailed explanation of community rights can be found on the author's blog: http://justinmbrant.blogspot.com/

9. Next, tick the **Accept SNMP packets from these hosts** radio button.

10. Click on the **Add** button underneath the radio buttons and add the IP of the server you have designated as the SolarWinds SAM host.

11. Once you complete these steps, the SNMP **Service Properties Security** tab should look something like the following screenshot. Notice that we used **192.168.1.3**, as that is the IP of the server where we plan to deploy SolarWinds SAM.

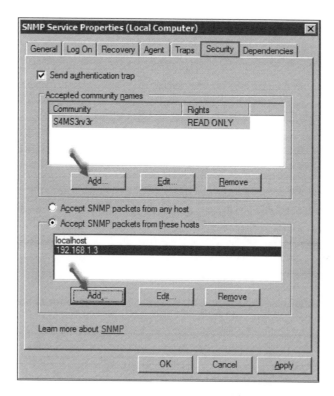

# Enabling and configuring WMI on Windows

Procedures in this section will ensure accessibility to WMI information by first enabling the service, followed by an outline of the creation process for a WMI service account.

# Enabling a WMI service on Windows

The following steps will ensure that the WMI service is always running:

1. Log in to a Windows server or desktop.

2. Navigate to **Start Menu** | **Control Panel** | **Administrative Tools** | **Services**.

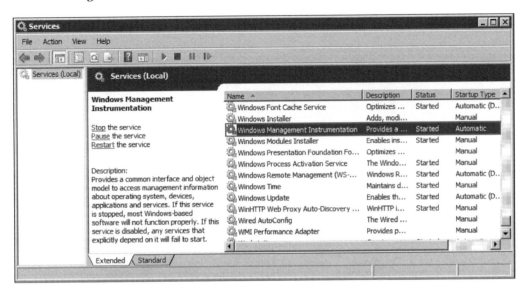

3. Check to see if the **Windows Management Instrumentation** service is running.

4. If it is not running, right-click on the **Windows Management Instrumentation** service and select **Properties**.

5. On the **General** tab, select **Automatic** under **Startup type**.

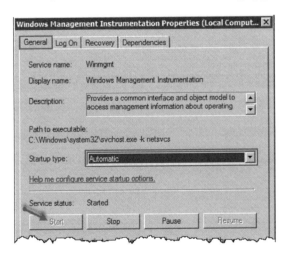

6. If necessary, click on the **Start** button, to start the service.
7. Click on **OK**.

# Creating an Active Directory service account for WMI

This procedure explains how to create an **Active Directory** (**AD**) user account, to act as a service account; used for SolarWinds SAM to poll your devices via WMI. These credentials will be used during and after SolarWinds SAM deployment.

1. Log in to a **Domain Controller** (**DC**) and launch AD.

2. Navigate to **Start Menu | Control Panel | Administrative Tools | Active Directory Users and Computers**.

3. Click on the **Users** container, or a container of your choice.

> To enhance our control and visibility over service accounts, we chose to use a container named **Managed Service Accounts**. This is optional.

4. Navigate to **Actions | New | User**.

5. Choose a **User logon name**. For example, we used SAMWMI.

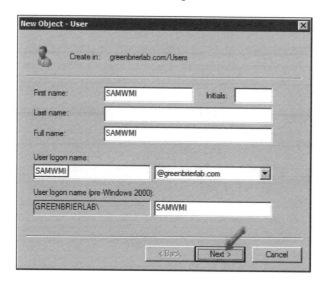

6. Click on **Next**.

7. Choose a secure **password**.

   ○   It is convenient to select **Password never expires**.

 It can be troublesome if a service account's password expires. If you choose for the password to expire, then we recommend setting up a calendar reminder to notify you when the service account password is nearing expiration, and then make the necessary adjustments to the account and to SolarWinds SAM.

   ○   This service account will have domain administrator privileges; make sure the password is very secure.

8. Click on **Finish**.

9. Double-click on the new user.

10. Select the **Member Of** tab.

11. Click on the **Add** button.

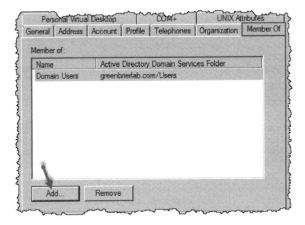

12. Type Domain Admins and click on the **Check Names** button. As shown in the following screenshot, if successful, **Domain Admins** will now be underlined.

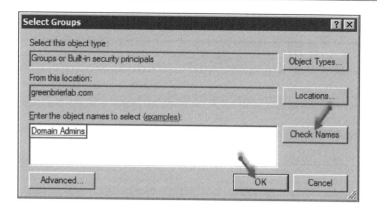

13. Click on **OK** to save and close the **Select Groups** window.

14. Click on **OK** to save and close the **Properties** window.

 We do not recommend using your own domain admin account, or any user account, for WMI authentication. Security is the primary reason. Your account may also become locked out due to failed password attempts, or your password may need to be changed, consequently breaking the SolarWinds WMI polling functionality.

This procedure is the easiest approach to quickly begin utilizing WMI for polling purposes.

Once you have worked your way through this book, and have SolarWinds SAM configured to your liking, we recommend that you research and implement one of the more complex (secure) methods.

 Procedures for creating an unprivileged WMI service account are referenced on the author's blog: http://justinmbrant. blogspot.com/

# VMware host monitoring prerequisites

This section discusses configuring your **Virtual Machine Hosts (VMHost)** for SolarWinds SAM integration. Procedures will outline how to enable **Secure Shell (SSH)** and SNMP on a VMHost, and then walk through the creation process of a VMware service account.

Ideally, you should also monitor each virtual server within a VMHost via SNMP or WMI. **VMware Tools** should be installed on all virtual servers. Note that the free version of VMware ESXi does not support SNMP.

# Enabling and configuring SNMP

There are a variety of ways to enable and configure SNMP on a VMHost. We will explain two methods, which should cover most VMHost types and versions. The first method only applies to VMware ESXi 5.1 and explains how to remotely enable SNMP via SSH. The second method involves logging in to the VMHost console itself, and should translate well to most versions.

## Method 1 – enabling and configuring SNMP via Secure Shell

There are two parts to this method; first we will enable SSH on the VMHost, and then use **PuTTY** to connect to the host and edit its `snmp.xml` file.

 PuTTY is a free open source terminal emulator that supports network protocols, such as SSH, SCP, Telnet, and rlogin. We will be using SSH in this procedure. Download PuTTY from the following URL: `http://www.putty.org/`

## Part 1 of 2 – enabling SSH on ESXi 5.1 using vSphere

The following steps explain how to enable SSH and open the firewall to allow SSH connections.

 We recommend only temporarily enabling SSH access, for security reasons.

1. Launch the **vSphere Client** and log in with administrator credentials, such as `root`.
2. Click on the **Inventory** icon in the **Inventory** panel.
3. In the left panel, select the **host**.
4. Click on the **Configuration** tab.
5. Click on **Security Profile** in the **Software** panel.

6. Click on **Properties** in the **Services** section.

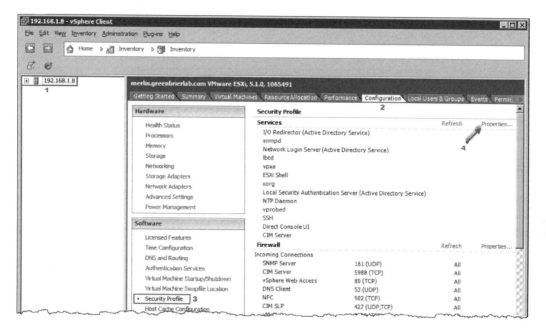

7. Select **SSH** in the **Service Properties** window.

8. Click on the **Options** button and select one of the following:

    ○ **Start and stop manually**: This enables temporary SSH access.

    ○ **Start and stop with host**: This enables SSH indefinitely. There are security implications to consider when enabling this feature.

9. Click on **Start** to enable the service.

10. Click on **OK** at the **SSH Options** window and the **Service Properties** window.

11. While still on the **Configuration** tab, select **Properties** in the **Firewall** section.

12. Check the box under **Required Services | Secure Shell | SSH Server**.

13. With **SSH Server** still selected, click on the **Firewall** button.

14. Select **Allow connections from any IP address** radio button and click on **OK**.

15. Click on **OK** at the **Firewall Properties** window.

## Part 2 of 2 – enabling and configuring SNMP using PuTTY

The following steps explains how to use PuTTY to connect to the host and edit its
`snmp.xml` file.

1. Run `putty.exe`.

 The author assumes that the reader is familiar with PuTTY. A detailed
tutorial for its use is beyond the scope of this book. For a PuTTY tutorial,
visit the author's blog at `http://justinmbrant.blogspot.com/`.

2. Connect to your VMHost. A command line window will appear.

3. Enter your `root` login credentials.

4. Click on **Yes** if you see a **PuTTY Security Alert**.

5. Navigate to the **VMware** folder:

   ```
   ~ # cd /etc/vmware
   /etc/vmware #
   ```

6. List folder contents to ensure `snmp.xml` is available:

   ```
   /etc/VMware/ # ls
   ```

7. Edit `snmp.xml` using **vi editor**:

   ```
   /etc/VMware # vi snmp.xml
   ```

8. You will see a single line; press *I* to enter the edit mode and use the arrow
   keys to navigate.

9. Enable SNMP by changing `false` to `true` between `<enable>` and `</enable>`.

10. Assign the community string by entering one between `<communities>` and
    `</communities>`. For example, we used *S4MVMH0st!*

```
192.168.1.8 - PuTTY                                                    _ □ X
<config><snmpSettings><enable>true</enable><communities>S4MVMH0st!</communities>
~
~
~
~
~
I snmp.xml 0/0 100%
```

11. Press *Esc* and type :wq to save and quit. If you made a mistake, type :q! to quit without saving, and repeat steps 6 through 12.

12. Restart the host daemon:

```
/etc /VMware/ # cd
~ # /etc/init.d/hostd restart
watchdog-hostd: Terminating watchdog process with PID 201623
hostd stopped.
hostd started.
```

 After successfully enabling and configuring SNMP on a VMHost, you should go back and disable SSH, then close the firewall to disallow SSH access.

# Method 2 – enabling SNMP on ESXi 5.1 or prior via the console

This method explains how to enable SNMP via the VMware ESXi console, by directly logging in to the VMHost server.

1. Go to the ESXi console on the server itself, that is, not remote.

2. Press *Alt + F1* to access the hidden console.

3. If using **ESXi 5.1**, then skip to step 6.

4. If using versions prior to ESXi 5.1 then type unsupported in the hidden console and press *Enter*.

 You will not see any text you as you type the password.

5. You will see **Tech Support Mode** warning.

6. Type the root **Login Credentials**.

7. Now follow steps 6 to 12 outlined in the *Part 2 of 2 – enabling and configuring SNMP using PuTTY* section.

# Creating a service account for VMHost

Before SolarWinds SAM can start polling a VMHost, a service account should be created for it to use, opposed to using the root credentials. The following procedure will explain how to create a VMware service account, to pass along to SolarWinds SAM.

1. Launch the vSphere Client and log in with administrator credentials, such as root.

2. Click on **Ignore** if you are prompted with an **untrusted SSL certificate** warning.

3. In the left panel select the host.

4. Select the **Local Users & Groups** tab in the right panel

5. Click on the **Users** button under view.

6. Right-click within the right panel, and then select **Add**.

7. On the **Add New User** window:

   ° Enter both a **Login** and a **User Name**. For example, we used SAMVMHOST.

   ° Enter and confirm a **Password**.

   ° Click on **OK**.

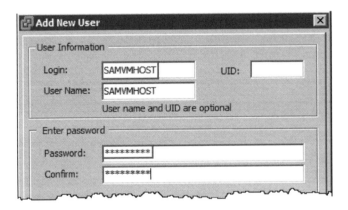

8. Select the **Permissions** tab.

9. Right-click within the right panel, and then select **Add Permission**.

10. On the **Assign Permissions** window, click on **Add**.

11. Click on the **Add** button.

12. Select the user you just created and click on **Add**, then click on **OK** on the **Select Users and Groups** window.

13. Under the **Assigned Role** area, select **Read-only** and then click on **OK** on the **Assign Permissions** window.

# Enabling and configuring SNMP on Cisco devices

Switches, routers, and firewalls should also be monitored, as they are crucial to the uptime of a network. This section covers command line procedures to enable and configure SNMP on some common Cisco devices.

Due to a wide range of manufactures and models, with varying configurations, your organization may use devices that are not listed in procedures referenced in this section. If that is the case, you should consult the manufacturer's website or user's manual.

Most vendors (including Cisco) ship equipment with these default SNMP community strings:

- `public` for read-only
- `private` for read-write
- `secret` for read-write-all

It is important to change these defaults due to security implications.

# Enabling and configuring SNMP on a Cisco switch

This procedure explains how to enable and configure SNMP on a Cisco 3550 switch running IOS version 12.1(20)EA1a.

1. Telnet to the switch (replace `192.168.1.230` with your switch IP):

   ```
   C:\>telnet 192.168.1.230
   ```

You can Telnet with PuTTY, explained in above referenced procedures; or if Telnet is installed, you can use Windows' Command Prompt method explained in step 1 of this procedure.

2. The **Password** field will appear. Enter the switch administrator password.

3. Type `enable` at the prompt and enter the enable password:

```
3550>enable
Password:
3550#
```

4. Enter the configuration terminal:

```
3550#configure terminal
Enter configuration commands, one per line. End with CTRL/Z.
3550(config)#
```

5. Enable the read-only community string:

```
3550(config)#snmp-server community S4MCisco3550SW1 RO
```

   ○   In this example, S4MCisco3550SW1 is the SNMP community string. You should choose your own community string.

   ○   To assign read-write rights, simply change RO to RW.

6. Designate SolarWinds SAM as the host network monitoring service:

```
3550(config)#snmp-server host 192.168.1.3 version 2c
S4MCisco3550SW1
```

In this command, `host 192.168.1.3` is the IP of our SolarWinds SAM server, `version 2c` designates SNMPv2C and `S4MCisco3550S1` references the new SNMP community string.

7. Exit the configuration terminal to save, and then verify the new SNMP community string:

```
3550(config)#exit
3550#show running-configuration
```

To remove an SNMP community string, or host network monitoring service, insert no in front of the commands listed in step 4 or 5. This is necessary if you made a typo.

# Enabling and configuring SNMP on a Cisco router

This procedure explains how to enable and configure SNMP on Cisco router; it is also applicable to a **Cisco IOS software-based XL Catalyst Switch**.

1. Telnet to the router (replace `192.168.1.1` with your router IP):

   ```
   prompt#telnet 192.168.1.1
   ```

2. Type `enable` at the prompt and enter the router administrator password:

   ```
   Router>enable
   Password:
   Router#
   ```

3. Display the running configuration to review the current SNMP information:

   ```
   Router#show running-config
   Building configuration...
   ....
   ....
   ```

4. Enable the configuration mode:

   ```
   Router#configure terminal
   Enter configuration commands, one per line. End
   with CNTL/Z.
   Router(config)#
   ```

5. Enable the read-only community string:

   ```
   Router(config)#snmp-server community public RO
   ```

   ○ In this example, `public` is the SNMP community string. You should change it to something more secure.

   ○ In this example, `RO` specifies read-only rights. To assign read-write rights, simply replace `RO` with `RW`.

6. Type `exit` to return to the main prompt:

   ```
   Router(config)#exit
   ```
   ```
   Router#
   ```

7. Type `write memory`, to save the settings:

   ```
   Router#write memory
   Building configuration...
   [OK]
   Router#
   ```

# Summary

You have prepared your environment for a network monitoring service. Next, we will utilize these services and protocols by deploying and configuring SolarWinds SAM.

In this chapter, we successfully:

- Enabled and configured SNMP and WMI on Windows Servers
- Created a WMI service account
- Enabled and configured SNMP and credentials on VMware ESXi
- Created a VMware service account
- Enabled and configured SNMP on common Cisco devices

# 2
# Installing and Configuring SolarWinds SAM

After enabling the monitoring services on your nodes and creating service accounts, SolarWinds SAM should be installed on a supported version of the Windows server. Following installation, the **Orion web console** will launch in the host server's default web browser. This interface will be used for most administrative tasks in SolarWinds SAM. Upon first log in, **Network Sonar Wizard (NSW)** will start.

This chapter will walk you through deploying SolarWinds SAM, ensure it is a smooth process, and help answer any questions that you may have along the way.

 Depending on the size of your network, it may be advantageous to install SolarWinds SAM and SQL on separate servers. For the purpose of this book, we will install both SolarWinds SAM and SQL on the same server.

## Installing SolarWinds SAM

This is a quick guide for installing SolarWinds SAM and all Windows server prerequisites. Ensure that all the recommended Windows updates are installed before proceeding.

1. Download the product from SolarWinds.com. If you have physical media, insert the CD or DVD and skip to step 4.

    1. Click on **PRODUCTS**.

    2. Select **Server & Application Monitor**.

    3. Click on **DOWNLOAD FREE TRIAL** (fully functional 30-day trial).

2. Unzip the installation package and run the executable.

3. If Microsoft .NET Framework 3.5 Service Pack 1 and 4.0 are not installed on your Windows server, then click on **Install**.

4. If you downloaded the software, confirm the e-mail address you provided while registering and click on **OK**.

5. Select **Yes** or **No** to sending anonymous data to SolarWinds.

6. Click on **Continue with Orion Installation. (Recommended)** to install IIS automatically during installation.

7. Review the license agreement, check **I accept the terms of the License Agreement**, and click on **Next**.

8. Choose your preferred destination folder and click on **Next**.

9. Select **Express Install** or **Advanced Install. Advanced Install** is for use with an existing SQL server database. We are using **Express Install**; this will install SQL, and then create and mount the SolarWinds SAM database.

10. Click on **Next** and proceed to **Start Copying Files**.

11. If necessary, the additional prerequisites will be installed (that is, C++, SQL, and IIS).

12. **Configuring Orion** will automatically start. If you selected **Express Install**, then the database will be created. In addition, the Orion web console website will be created via IIS.

13. Click on **Finish**.

# Configuring SolarWinds SAM

Following a successful installation, the Orion web console will automatically launch in your server's default web browser.

Log in to the interface using admin as the **User name** and leave the **Password** field empty.

Do not use the browser's back button while using the Orion web console.

Upon first log in, NSW will begin. We recommend that you complete the wizard, as it will save some time by enabling the SolarWinds SAM's "out-of-the-box" functionality.

Make note of the Windows server hostname (that is, computer name) where SolarWinds SAM resides; you can easily log in to the Orion web console from any network computer by using `http://hostname:8787/` and replacing the hostname with your SolarWinds SAM server.

# Network Sonar Wizard

This wizard will help populate the SolarWinds SAM database with:

- **Simple Network Management Protocol (SNMP)** nodes
- **vCenter, ESX,** or **ESXi** hosts (VMHosts)
- **Windows Management Instrumentation (WMI)** nodes
- **Internet Control Message Protocol (ICMP)** via scanning and discovering IP ranges or subnets for additional nodes
- Applications

*Chapter 3, Customizing SolarWinds SAM,* will explain how to manually accomplish everything which NSW provides.

# The SNMP page

Start by entering the preconfigured SNMP credentials to add servers and devices. Enabling and configuring nodes for SNMP is covered in the *Enabling and configuring SNMP on Windows* section of *Chapter 1, Deployment Strategy.*

Click on **Add New Credential** and enter one **SNMP Community String** per device, and then click on **ADD**. For example, we used s4MS3rv3r in the *Assigning a SNMP community string on Windows* section of the previous chapter.

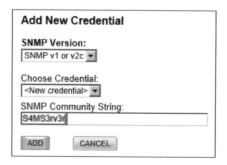

Once you have finished adding all SNMP nodes, click on **NEXT** to progress to the **VMware** page.

# The VMware page

Add VMHost credentials to SolarWinds SAM for centralizing polling data within the Orion web console. Creating VMHost credentials is covered in the *Creating service account for VMHost* section of *Chapter 1, Deployment Strategy*.

Click on **Add vCenter or ESX Credential** to add a VMHost; **Credential Name** is a "friendly name" used to differentiate between multiple VMHosts. Enter a **User Name** and **Password** for a VMHost service account, and then click on **ADD**. For example, we use SAMVMHOST, as used in the previously mentioned section, and go with VMHost 1 for the "friendly credential name."

Click on **NEXT** to progress to the **Windows** page.

# The Windows page

From the **Windows** page, WMI credentials can be assigned by entering service account credentials. Creating a service account and enabling the WMI service is explained in the *Enabling and configuring WMI on Windows* section of *Chapter 1, Deployment Strategy*. Later the NSW will perform a network scan and SolarWinds SAM will automatically detect nodes with WMI enabled, and use your WMI service account for authentication.

 You cannot simultaneously poll a network node with both SNMP and WMI. You can change between the two, but you must choose one at a time.

If you wish to utilize WMI for polling, click on **Add New Credential**, and enter a **User Name** and **Password** for a WMI service account credential, and then click on **Add**. **Credential Name** is a "friendly name" for the purpose of having multiple WMI service accounts. For example, we use SAMWMI, from the *Creating an Active Directory service account for WMI* section of *Chapter 1, Deployment Strategy*, and go with WMI 1 for the "friendly credential name."

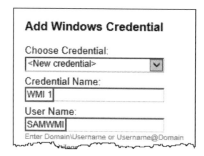

Click on **NEXT** to progress to the **Network** page.

# The Network page

This feature is designed to scan and discover nodes via **IP Ranges**, **Subnets**, or **Specific Nodes**. Use this to scan your entire network or refine the scan to specific areas within your network. For example, we chose to scan by IP ranges 192.168.1.1 through 192.168.1.254.

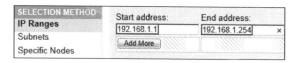

Make your selections and click on **NEXT** to progress to the **Discovery Settings** page.

# The Discovery Settings page

The **Discovery Settings** page is intended for customizing the subsequent **Discovering Network...** scan. Default settings normally suffice.

 You may choose to select **Ignore nodes that only respond to ICMP (ping). Nodes must respond to SNMP, WMI.** We will leave this option **unchecked**, because we plan to promote all applicable ICMP nodes to SNMP or WMI, after NSW finishes.

Click on **NEXT** to progress to **Discovery Scheduling**.

# The Discovery Scheduling page

**Discovery Scheduling** is designed to automatically scan your network at scheduled intervals. To preserve bandwidth, we recommend manually adding nodes, or manually scanning your network, unless you frequently add/remove nodes, and want to be "hands-off" in regards to SolarWinds SAM administration.

We select **Once** from the **Frequency** dropdown and **Yes, run this discovery now** in the **Execute immediately** radio buttons.

Click on **Discover** to begin the **Discovering Network...** scan.

 Once the scan begins, do not click on **CANCEL**, as it may crash NSW and cause problems with the Orion web console.

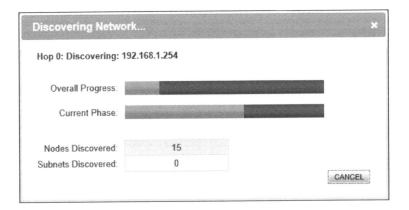

 **Discovering Network...** scan time will vary depending on the size of your network.

Once **Discovering Network...** finishes, discovered servers and devices are displayed on the **Network Sonar Results Wizard** page.

## The Network Sonar Results Wizard page

This section of NSW will contain discovered nodes (results) captured during the **Discovering Network...** scan. Each subsequent page will progress through configuring and importing managed servers and devices.

# The Devices page

This page allows for custom selections of server and/or device types for importing into SolarWinds SAM. The choices made here will affect the subsequent import process.

Select your choices and click on **NEXT** to be taken to the **Interfaces** page and then to the **Volumes** page.

# The Volumes page

The **Volumes** page is intended for customization of volume types to monitor as per the devices selected previously. All these volume types require either SNMP or WMI enabled per device, as ICMP will not suffice for polling this type of data. Select what you feel to be appropriate for your environment. Generally, the default selections will be fine.

Click on **NEXT** to be taken to the **SAM Import Settings** page.

# The SAM Import Settings page

This page contains WMI Interface Status Settings. From here, choose which WMI interfaces will be imported. To clarify:

- **Operationally Up**: Nodes in an online state will be imported.
- **Operationally Down**: Nodes in an operationally down state (meaning not necessarily planned) will be imported. This is included because interfaces may intermittently cycle off and on.
- **Administratively Shutdown**: Meaning devices in a shutdown state (meaning planned) will be imported.

Click on **NEXT** to progress to the **Import Preview** page.

# The Import Preview page

This is the final step before importing nodes based off prior selections in NSW. You should review the polling method (that is, SNMP, WMI, or ICMP). It will be beneficial to promote the ICMP nodes to SNMP or WMI to poll for more comprehensive data. Remember that ICMP only pings nodes and collects status, response time, and packet loss data. Promoting nodes will be covered in *Chapter 3, Customizing SolarWinds SAM*.

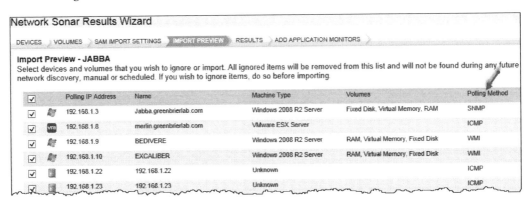

Choose to import everything or select specific nodes, and then click on **IMPORT** to start importing your selections into SolarWinds SAM.

After the process finishes, you will be taken to the **RESULTS** page, to review a log of the import results. Click on **NEXT** to be taken to the **Add Application Monitors** page.

 If you do not plan to import applications, then click on **FINISH** and skip to the *Active Directory integration* section in this chapter.

# Application Discovery

This portion of NSW is designed to automatically import pertinent applications, such as SQL, to be polled by SolarWinds SAM with SNMP. The servers listed on this page are dependent on your earlier selections in NSW. Your selections will be scanned for applications designed for a network monitoring service.

Click on **NEXT** to progress to the **Select Applications** page.

## The Select Applications page

From the **Applications** page select all or specific applications and types to scan for. You can modify the **Show only** drop-down menu to display more than just **Popular** applications.

Make your selections and click on **NEXT** to progress to the **Enter Credentials** page.

## The Enter Credentials page

This page is intended for applications that require credentials for polling. The following steps will help you achieve this:

1. Click on **Add Credential** to add application credentials.
2. Click on **NEXT** to progress to the **REVIEW & START SCAN** page. Review your selections and click on **START SCAN**.

After **Application Discovery** finishes, you will be asked if you wish to add UX (user experience) monitors. Click on **NO, ADD UX MONITORS LATER**.

This concludes NSW and takes us to the Orion web console home page.

# Active Directory integration

The most practical way to administer and monitor SolarWinds SAM is through Orion web console, since it is accessible from any computer on your network. Depending on the size of your organization, there may be more than one individual who needs access to Orion web console. Certain individuals may also require less than administrative privileges.

For example, some users may need *Guest* rights, to allow viewing data, but remain prohibited from making changes. You may also choose to isolate specific IT departments or users to applicable nodes, such as isolating the telecom department to telecom-related nodes. Therefore, the most efficient route is to grant permission through AD integration.

This section will outline how to use AD for access control to Orion web console.

Procedures explain how to create a security group for granting administrative privileges, and then apply the group to your own domain account, followed by creating a required SolarWinds SAM access control service account.

You can modify these procedures to create additional security groups (as needed), to limit users to specific areas and features within the Orion web console. Only one access control service account is necessary.

# Creating a security group for SolarWinds SAM

This procedure explains how to create an AD security group for the purpose of granting administrative permissions to the Orion web console.

1. Log in to a Domain Controller (DC) or launch AD from a desktop that has RSAT tools installed.

2. Navigate to **Start** | **Control Panel** | **Administrative Tools** | **Active Directory Users and Computers**.

3. Click on the **Users** container, or a container of your choice.

To enhance control and visibility over service accounts, we chose to use a container named **Managed Service Accounts**. This is optional.

4. Naviagte to **Actions** | **New** | **Group**.

5. Enter a **Group name** and ensure that the **Security** and **Global** radio buttons are selected. For example, we used SAM Admins.

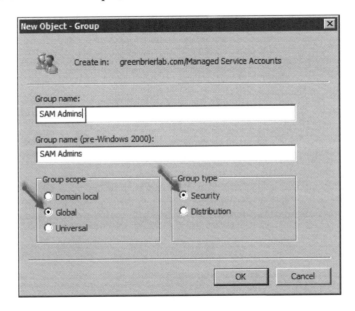

6. Click on **OK**.

7. Now simply open your own AD **User Account**, select the **Member Of** tab, click on **Add**, and type the name of the **security group** (for example, SAM Admins).

# Creating a service account for SolarWinds SAM

SolarWinds SAM requires a privileged account before assigning a security group for access control to the Orion web console. You can use the same procedures as used in the *Creating an Active Directory service account for WMI* section of *Chapter 1, Deployment Strategy*, and name this account something applicable. For example, we went with SAMAdmins.

# Assigning a security group to SolarWinds SAM

Now that a SAM Admins security group and a SAMAdmin service account have been created, they need to be associated with SolarWinds SAM. This procedure shows how.

1. Log in to the **Orion web console**.

2. Click on **Settings** in the upper right-hand corner of the screen.

3. Click on **Manage Accounts** under the **User Accounts** section.

4. Click on the **Groups** tab.

5. Click on **Add New Group Account**.

6. Type the **User Name** and **Password** of the SolarWinds SAM service account. For example, we used **greenbrierlab\SAMAdmin**.

7. Type the **Group name** of the SolarWinds SAM administrators security group and click on the **Search** button. For example, we used **greenbrierlab\ SAM Admins**.

8. The security group will appear under **ADD GROUPS**. Select it and click on **NEXT**.

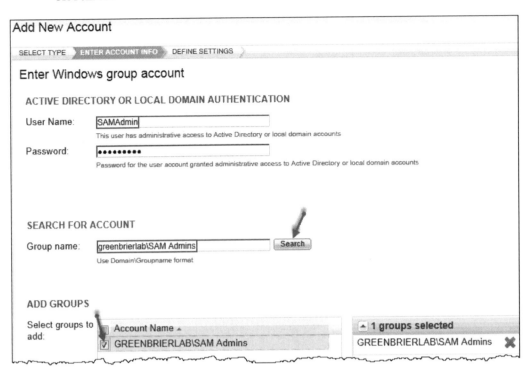

From the **Edit Account** page, a wide range of Orion web console access control settings can be manipulated. The following **Edit Account** page settings are applicable to a SolarWinds SAM administrator account:

1. Change **Allow Administrator Rights** to **Yes**.

2. Change **Allow Node Management Rights** to **Yes**.

3. Change **Allow Account to Customize Views** to **Yes**.

4. Change **Allow Account to Clear Events, Acknowledge Alerts and Syslogs** to **Yes**.

5. Change **Allow Browser Integration** to **Yes**.

6. Expand **Server & Application Monitor Settings** and change **SAM User Role** to **Admin**.

7. Change **Real-Time Process Explorer** to **Full Control**.

8. Check **Service Control Manager**.

9. Check **Allow Service Actions Rights**.

10. Check **Allow nodes to be rebooted**.

11. Click on the **Submit** button.

 Test everything by logging out of the Orion web console and logging in with your AD credentials.

# Summary

After successfully deploying SolarWinds SAM, completing the NSW, and enabling AD access control, a foundation has been established for tailoring your new network monitoring service to your environment.

In this chapter, we covered:

- Downloading the SolarWinds SAM 30-day trial
- Installing SolarWinds SAM on Windows Server 2008 R2
- Configuring SolarWinds SAM for basic network monitoring services
- Integrating Active Directory for access control to the Orion web console

# 3

# Customizing SolarWinds SAM

After deploying SolarWinds SAM, nodes that were missed during the **Network Sonar Wizard (NSW)** should be manually added. You may decide to monitor everything network wide, or for bandwidth conservation you may choose to exclude the low priority nodes. Therefore it may be necessary to remove, disable, or demote nodes.

By now it should be clear that **Internet Control Message Protocol (ICMP)** is not the preferred method for polling, because it does not empower SolarWinds SAM to poll inclusive data. For that reason it is recommended to promote applicable ICMP nodes to SNMP or WMI. Remember that SolarWinds SAM uses SNMP and WMI in conjunction with ICMP, meaning that promoted nodes will not exclude status, response time, or packet loss polling data.

To ensure service levels are met through high availability and overall awareness of IT services, all nodes should be classified, prioritized, and grouped. Classifying or grouping nodes by type will also assist in asset management and streamlining administrative tasks, and allow you to visualize the physical location of servers and devices. The ability to easily identify nodes is imperative in the event of an outage or depreciation of service, to expeditiously pinpoint and identify the core issue.

This chapter will provide procedures for everything listed above; it is designed to teach you how to customize and tailor SolarWinds SAM to your network environment.

# Manually adding nodes

This section will include procedures outlining how to manually add servers, devices, VMHosts, and applications to SolarWinds SAM. This is in contrast to automatically scanning and detecting nodes, which will be covered later in this chapter. Depending on the size of your network environment, this manual approach may be the best practice for bandwidth conservation and importing nodes promptly, without scanning an entire subnet.

# Adding servers and devices

The following procedure explains how to manually add a node to be polled with SNMPv2c.

 When adding a virtual node hosted on a VMHost, it is recommended to have **VMware Tools** installed on the machine for additional polling information.

1. Log in to the Orion web console.
2. Navigate to **Orion Website Administration** by clicking on **Settings** in the upper-right corner of the browser window.
3. Click on Manage Nodes under Node & Group Management.
4. Click on **Add Node** in the toolbar.

5. From the **Define Node** page, enter the **Polling Hostname or IP Address** of the node you wish to poll. For example, we added our Cisco Catalyst 3550 Switch by entering IP `192.168.1.251`.
6. Select **Most Devices: SNMP and ICMP - Recommended**.
7. Enter the preconfigured SNMP **Community String**.

 The default **Port 161** will normally suffice for **SNMPv2c**. If you run into issues, consult the device manufacture's website or user manual.

8. Click on the **Test** button underneath **Read/Write Community String**. If the community string is valid, you will see **Test Successful!**.
9. Click on **NEXT**.

10. Optionally, from the **Add Application Monitors** page, you can add an application. This only applies if the node you added in step 6 is a server that contains application(s) that have integrated network monitoring capabilities. Manually and automatically adding applications will be covered later in this chapter.

11. Click on **NEXT**.

12. Optionally, from the **Change Properties** page, you can change the friendly **Name** of the server or device. For example, we changed `192.168.1.251` to `Cisco Catalyst 3550 Switch`. **Custom Properties** can also be assigned at this time, and will be covered in detail later in this chapter.

13. Click on **OK, Add Node**.

This procedure can also apply to adding a **Status Only** (ICMP) or **Windows Server** (WMI) node, by modifying step 6.

• For a WMI node, select **Windows Servers** and use the drop-down menu to choose a preconfigured WMI credential. Refer to the service account created in the *Creating an Active Directory service account for WMI* section of *Chapter 1, Deployment Strategy*, and added as a WMI credential in *The Windows page* section of *Chapter 2, Installing and Configuring SolarWinds SAM*.

• For an ICMP ping-only node, select **Status Only**; no additional configuration is required.

# Adding VMHosts

The following procedure explains how to add a VMHost by using SNMP and a VMware service account.

1. Log in to the Orion web console.

2. Navigate to **Orion Website Administration** by clicking on **Settings**.

3. Click on **Manage Nodes** under **Node & Group Management**.

4. Click on **Add Node** in the toolbar.

5. From the **Define Node** page enter the **Polling Hostname or IP Address** of the VMHost you wish to poll. For example, we added our VMware ESXi 5.1 Host by entering IP `192.168.1.8`.

6. Enter the preconfigured VMHost SNMP **Community String**. For example, we used `S4MVMHOst!`.

7. Click on the **Test** button underneath **Read/Write Community String**. If the community string is valid, you will see **Test Successful!**.

8. Check the box next to **Poll for VMware** under **Additional Monitoring Options**.

9. Click on the drop-down menu under **vCenter or ESX credentials** and select a VMHost service account credential. Refer to the Service Account created in the *Creating a service account for VMHost* section of *Chapter 1, Deployment Strategy*, and added as a VMHost credential in *The VMware page* section of *Chapter 2, Installing and Configuring SolarWinds SAM*.

10. Click on the **Test** button underneath **Confirm password**. If the service account credentials are valid then you will see **Test Successful!**

11. Click on **NEXT**.

The following screenshot sequentially illustrates the steps outlined in this procedure.

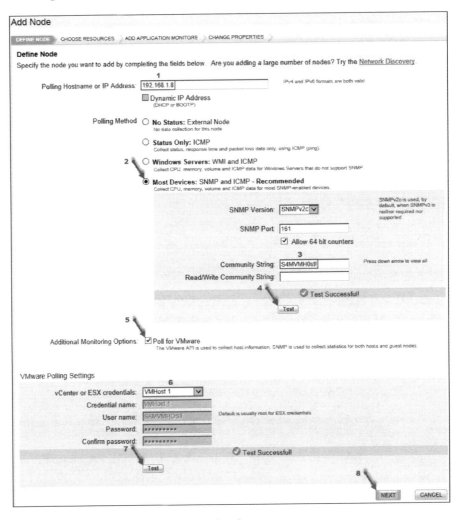

1. The **Choose Resources** page will appear. From here you can select what will be polled.

2. Click on **NEXT** at the **Add Application Monitors** page.

3. Optionally, from the **Change Properties** page, you can change the friendly **Name** of the VMHost. For example, we changed `192.168.1.8` to `VMware ESXi 5.1 VMHost 1`. **Custom Properties** can also be assigned at this time.

4. Click on **OK, Add Node**.

# Adding application monitors to nodes

In order to monitor an application, servers containing pertinent applications must first be added to SolarWinds SAM. Servers must be configured to be polled by WMI or SNMP and then told to monitor specific applications. For most Microsoft applications, such as IIS, the server node will need to be polled with WMI.

For application monitoring SolarWinds SAM uses **Application Templates**, which are made up of predefined **Component Monitors**. These are advanced customizable features; it is not essential to use them, as the pre-configured application monitors included out of the box are sufficient to effectively monitor your network.

In most cases, manually adding servers and devices is generally the way to go; however, **Discovery Central** (explained in the next section of this chapter) tends to be more efficient for adding applications.

The following procedure explains how to manually add applications hosted on previously added server nodes.

1. Log in to the Orion web console.

2. Navigate to **Orion Website Administration** by clicking on **Settings**.

3. Click on **SAM Settings** under **Settings**.

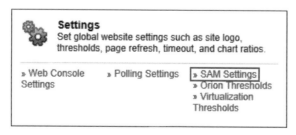

4. Click on **Manually Assign Application Monitors** under **Getting Started with SAM**.

5.  From the **Select Template** tab, select the application that you wish to monitor. For example, we selected **Internet Information Service (IIS) Services and Counters**.

6.  Click on **NEXT**.

7.  From the **Select Nodes** tab, select the server node that you would like to add the application monitor to and click on the green arrow button to move it to the **Selected Nodes** pane. For example, we selected our SolarWinds SAM server **Jabba.greenbrierlab.com**.

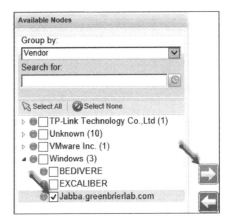

8.  Check the box next to the server node you added to the **Selected Nodes** right pane.

9.  Click on **NEXT**.

10. From the **Select Credentials & Test** tab, select the credentials you would like to use. For example, we selected **Inherit Windows credentials from node** to use our WMI service account credentials that provide authentication to poll **Jabba.greenbrierlab.com**.

 Database credentials may differ from WMI service account credentials (that is, **Inherit Windows credentials from node**). If this is the case then select **Assign custom credential**, and enter the database credentials.

11. Click on **Test**.

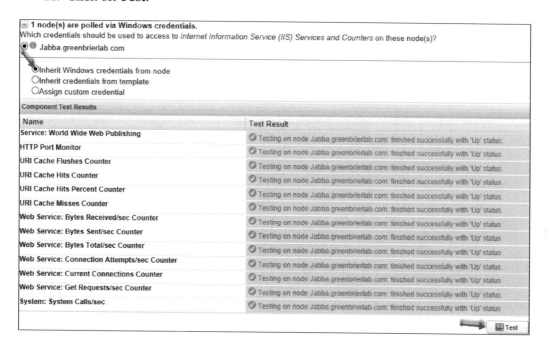

12. If the test results were successful, click on the **Assign Application Monitors** button.

13. Click on **Done**.

# Discovery Central

Automatically scanning and detecting nodes with **Network Sonar Discovery** is useful for adding groups of nodes. **Application Discovery** also makes it possible to scan and detect applications. If you frequently add or remove nodes, then you can configure the frequency of these scans to run on predetermined schedules.

These procedures will explain automated node and application discovery.

# Network Sonar Discovery

Automatically scanning your network for nodes and/or applications is accomplished by running a discovery profile. The following procedure explains how to run or make changes to the discovery profile that was created and configured during the NSW in *The Network Sonar Results Wizard page* section of *Chapter 2, Installing and Configuring SolarWinds SAM.*

1.  Log in to the Orion web console.

2.  Navigate to **Orion Website Administration** by clicking on **Settings**.

3.  Click on **Network Sonar Discovery** under **Getting Started with Orion**.

4.  If you have completed the NSW then select your discovery profile.

>  The discovery profile will be titled something like **admin: <date>, <time>**.

5.  Click on **Discover Now**, in the toolbar.

6.  If there have been changes made to your network after completing the NSW, then you can reconfigure your discovery profile by selecting it and clicking on **Edit** in the toolbar. For example, your company may have a new building with a new subnet that you need to add to the IP Ranges of your **Discovery Settings**. By editing the profile you can also adjust the scan frequency (for automated scheduled networks scans).

7.  If you have not yet completed the NSW then click on **Add New Discovery** in the toolbar, and refer to *The Network Sonar Results Wizard* page section of *Chapter 2, Installing and Configuring SolarWinds SAM* for step by step instructions and examples.

# Application Discovery

The following procedure explains how to automatically scan for applications:

1.  Log in to the Orion web console.

2.  Navigate to **Orion Website Administration** by clicking on **Settings**.

3.  Click on **Discovery Central** under **Getting Started with Orion**.

4.  Click on the **Discover Applications** button under **Application Discovery**.

5. Step by step procedures are covered in the *Application Discovery* section of *Chapter 2, Installing and Configuring SolarWinds SAM*.

# Removing nodes and disabling polling

This section covers how to remove nodes or applications entirely from the SolarWinds SAM database, and how to disable nodes, allowing nodes to remain accessible but excluded from polling.

 You can select multiple nodes during these procedures.

# Removing a node from SolarWinds SAM

The following procedure explains how to completely remove a node; it will be removed from the SolarWinds SAM SQL database and will no longer be displayed in the Orion web console:

1. Log in to the Orion web console.
2. Navigate to **Orion Website Administration** by clicking on **Settings**.
3. Click on **Manage Nodes** under **Node & Group Management**.
4. Select a node by checking the box next to it. Do not click on the node itself because that will take you to the **Node Details Summary** page.
5. Click on the **Delete** button in the upper-right corner of the toolbar.

6. You will be prompted with **Are you sure you want to delete the selected item?**.
7. Click on **Yes**.

# Disabling a node from data polling

The following procedure outlines how to stop a node from being polled by SolarWinds SAM. The primary reason to do this is to conserve the bandwidth by disabling the low priority nodes, yet still allow these nodes to be managed by SolarWinds SAM.

You can also stop polling a node and still receive SNMP trap and Syslog data from it, covered in *Chapter 4, Events, Traps, and Alerts*, and *Chapter 5, Syslog, Reporting, and Network Atlas.*

1. Log in to the Orion web console.
2. Navigate to **Orion Website Administration** by clicking on **Settings**.
3. Click on **Manage Nodes** under **Node & Group Management**.
4. Select a node by checking the box next to it.
5. Click on **Edit Properties**.

6. Select **No Status: External Node**.
7. Click on **Submit**.

# Removing an application monitor

One disadvantage to automatically scanning with **Discovery Central** is that application monitors may have been added that are not necessary for your environment. The following procedure explains how to remove an application monitor from a server node:

1. Log in to the Orion web console.
2. Navigate to **Orion Website Administration** by clicking on **Settings**.
3. Click on **SAM Settings** under **Settings**.
4. Select **Manage Application Monitors** under **Application Monitors**.
5. Select an **Application Monitor** under the **Assigned Application Monitors** column.
6. Press the **Delete** button in the toolbar. This will remove the application monitor entirely.

# Disabling an application monitor from polling

To temporarily disable application polling, you can follow the steps given in the *Removing an application monitor* section of this chapter. In step 6, click on the **Unmanage** button in the toolbar. Then indicate the duration of time you wish for the application to be unmanaged. The green icon next to the application will change to a blue icon with an **X** through it, indicating that the application monitor is now **Unmanaged**. Polling and statistics collection will be suspended while applications are **Unmanaged**.

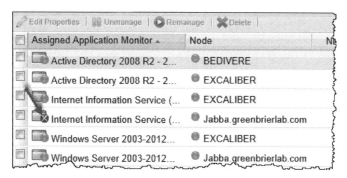

# Promoting nodes

As mentioned throughout this book, we recommend promoting your ICMP (ping-only) vital nodes to SNMP or WMI. Furthermore, you may want to change an SNMP node to WMI, or vice versa.

Remember that WMI takes roughly five times the bandwidth when compared to SNMP; but it provides some additional Windows-specific polling data. That said, WMI will not provide certain data that SNMP offers, such as the interface information. You have to decide for yourself if WMI is right for your environment; testing both SNMP and WMI is a good idea.

> Be cautious when changing polling methods from SNMP or WMI because you will lose all historical data that SolarWinds SAM previously gathered!

The following procedure explains how to promote an ICMP node to SNMP.

 You can select multiple nodes to promote during this procedure. When concurrently promoting multiple nodes to SNMP, the same **Community String** must be assigned to all selected nodes.

1. Log in to the Orion web console.
2. Navigate to **Orion Website Administration** by clicking on **Settings**.
3. Click on **Manage Nodes** under **Node & Group Management**.
4. Select a node by checking the box next to it. For example, we selected **TP LINK TL-SG2424 Switch**, which was detected automatically as ICMP and labeled **192.168.1.253** by the **Discovery Scan** in the *The Discovery Scheduling page* section of *Chapter 2, Installing and Configuring SolarWinds SAM*.
5. Click on **Edit Properties** in the toolbar.
6. Select **Most Devices: SNMP and ICMP - Recommended**.
7. Enter the preconfigured SNMP **Community String**.
8. Click on the **Test** button underneath **Read/Write Community String**. If the **Community String** is valid, you will see **Test Successful!**.
9. Click on **Submit**.
10. You can see the additional data that is being polled by promoting the node to SNMP by expanding the node via the **+** sign next to it.

This procedure can apply to promoting an ICMP node to WMI, or to switch between SNMP and WMI. Simply modify step 6 by selecting **Windows Servers** and use the drop-down menu to choose a preconfigured WMI credential.

Additionally, you can modify step 6 to demote SNMP or WMI nodes to ICMP.

# Classifying nodes

This procedure explains how to assign pertinent information to nodes, such as a device name, physical location, and/or the priority of the device. We recommend thoroughly labeling and categorizing all nodes to reflect your network environment; this will be beneficial later during administration, reporting, alerting, and so on. To a certain extent, this also empowers SolarWinds SAM to act as an asset management service for production servers, devices, and applications.

# Creating custom properties

This tutorial explains how to create a custom property that will include a drop-down list with information related to your organization. In this example we will create an **Address** custom property.

It is beneficial to take a well-planned and methodical approach when designing your custom properties structure. At this point, more work now means less work later, and greater overall SolarWinds SAM functionality.

1.  Log in to the Orion web console.
2.  Navigate to **Orion Website Administration** by clicking on **Settings**.
3.  Click on **Manage Custom Properties** under **Node & Group Management**.
4.  Click on the **Add Custom Property** button in the toolbar.

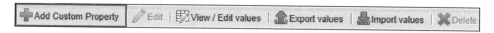

5.  Select **Nodes** from the drop-down list and click on **NEXT**.
6.  Select **Address** under **Property Templates**.
7.  Check the box next to **Create a custom drop-down list of values for this property**.

8. Add each building location in your organization and click on the **Add Value** button after each entry. For example, we added building addresses and included floor number within brackets to indicate the location of server rooms.

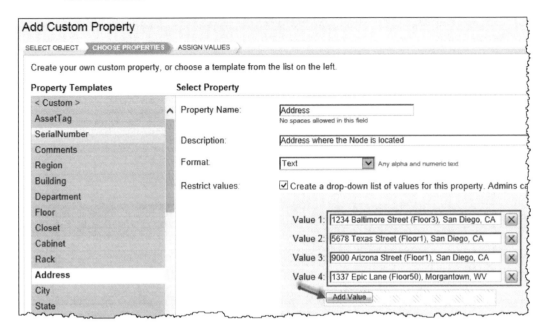

9. Once you are finished creating the drop-down list, click on **NEXT**.

10. You can choose to **Select Nodes** and associate them with the new custom property.

11. Click on **Submit**.

12. You should remove any default categories you do not find necessary. To do so, select a **Custom Property** and click on the **Delete** button in the toolbar. For example, since we created **Address** we removed **City**.

Other recommended custom properties includes the following:

- **DeviceType**: For example, **Server**, **Desktop**, and **Network Device**; specifying hardware types

- **Department**: For example, **Telecom**, **Network Operations Center**, and **Desktop Support**

- **Priority**: For example, **Low** (desktops), **Medium** (non-production servers), and **High** (vital devices)

# Applying custom properties

Creating custom properties may not be a necessity for all organizations; however, all nodes should still be labeled properly by device name. At minimum, these steps should be applied to all nodes labeled **Unknown** by the NSW discovery scan; an **Unknown** node will normally only display the IP address. In the event of an outage, it is detrimental to stop troubleshooting to figure out what the out-of-service device is.

The following procedure will explain how to label nodes and apply custom properties that are previously created.

> You can select multiple nodes during this procedure; you will not be able to change multiple node names concurrently, but you can apply custom properties to groups of nodes.

1. Log in to the Orion web console.
2. Navigate to **Orion Website Administration** by clicking on **Settings**.
3. Click on **Manage Nodes** under **Node & Group Management**.
4. By default, nodes are set as **Vendor** under **Group by:**; leave them grouped as **Vendor** for now and select the **Unknown** category.
5. Select a node by checking the box next to it. Choose one labeled only by internal IP. To name it appropriately you should know beforehand what the device or server actually is. For example, we selected **192.168.1.254**, our Cisco 2621 Router.
6. Click on **Edit Properties**.

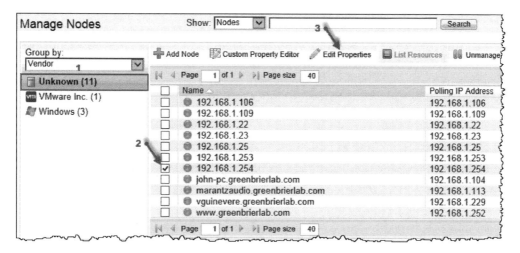

7. From the **Edit Properties** page, change the IP address to something easy to recognize by editing the **Name** field. For example, we changed the friendly name from **192.168.1.254** to Cisco 2621 Router.

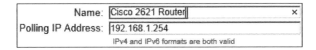

8. Optionally, under **Custom Properties** scroll down and assign properties that were created in the previous section. Use the drop-down menus to select all applicable properties. From this page you can also select **Add new value** to further populate your designated **Custom Properties**. For example, we selected all of our preconfigured custom properties, and added a new property to **DeviceType** called Router.

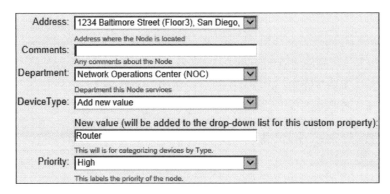

9. Click on **Submit** to save the changes.

# Managing groups

Groups provide a number of administrative benefits such as assisting with alerting, reporting, and dependencies. Groups will save you time and make you more efficient as a network or systems administrator. These procedures will explain how to create a group and then assign nodes to the group.

# Creating groups

The following procedure explains how to create a group. The group created here will be used in the *Creating reports* section of *Chapter 5, Syslog, Reporting, and Network Atlas*:

1. Log in to the Orion web console.

2. Navigate to **Orion Website Administration** by clicking on **Settings**.

3. Click on **Manage Groups** under **Node & Group Management**.

4. Click on **Add New Group**.

5. Choose a **Name** and **Description** for this new group under **Define Group Properties**. For example, we called our group Network Devices.

6. Optionally, you can expand the **Advanced** setting to adjust the **Status rollup mode**. The default selection is **Mixed** and the **Refresh frequency** default is **every 60 seconds**. The default settings will normally suffice.

7. Click on **NEXT**.

8. This takes you to the **Add Orion Objects to your new group** page. Select the nodes that you would like added to this group by checking the boxes next to them, and then click on the green arrow button labeled **Add to Group**. For example, we selected all network devices presently active in our network.

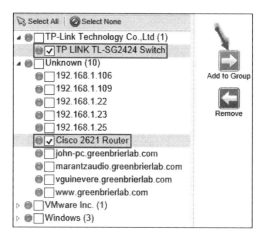

9. Click on the **Create Group** button.

# Modifying groups

The following procedure explains how to modify a group to add group members to it:

1. Log in to the Orion web console.

2. Navigate to **Orion Website Administration** by clicking on **Settings**.

3.  Click on **Manage Groups** under **Node & Group Management**.

4.  Select the group you wish to modify by checking the box next to it. If you click on the group itself, it will take you to **Group Details**.

5.  Click on **Edit Properties** in the toolbar.

6.  You can make adjustments to the **Name**, **Description**, or **Advanced** settings from the **Edit Group** page.

7.  Click on the **Add & Remove Objects** button under **Contains**.

8.  Check the boxes next to nodes that you wish to add or remove, and select **Add to Group** or **Remove** to move them to the appropriate pane.

9.  Click on **Submit**.

# Defining dependencies

In SolarWinds SAM dependencies are contingent on the topological layout of your network infrastructure. For example, if a switch goes down then nodes dependent on that switch will also be inaccessible. Defining dependencies is not required, although it will help pinpoint the core issue in the event of an outage, or when network related issues occur. The Orion web console provides a clear description of dependencies, as displayed in the following screenshot:

> **What are dependencies?** A child is dependent on a parent. The child will appear 'unreachable' instead of 'down' when the parent is down.
> **Why use dependencies?** Avoid a flood of down alerts when a central interface/node goes down, make reports more accurate. » Learn more

The following procedure will explain how to create and define a dependency.

1.  Log in to the Orion web console.

2.  Navigate to **Orion Website Administration** by clicking on **Settings**.

3.  Click on **Manage Dependencies** under **Node & Group Management**.

4.  Click on **Add new dependency** in the toolbar.

5.  From the **Select Parent** tab, select a device or server that has nodes that depend on it. For example, we selected our labeled **TP Link TL-SG2424 Switch**.

6.  Click on **NEXT**.

7. From the **Choose Child** tab, select the group of nodes or a node that depends on the server or device. For example, we sorted by the **Show Only:** field by **Groups** and selected our **Servers** group, since our servers depend on the **TP Link TL-SG2424 Switch** for connectivity.

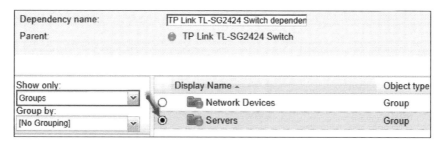

This is one of many processes where groups can come in handy. For example, hypothetically:

- Let's say this switch is the **Parent** for all **Servers** in `Building A` of your company
- Create a group labeled `Building A Servers`
- Easily populate the new group by sorting by the **Address** custom property of `Building A`
- In step 7 sort the **Show only:** field by **Groups**
- Then add the `Building A Servers` group

8. Click on **NEXT**.

9. Review your **Dependency Name**, **Parent object**, and **Child object**; then click on **Submit**.

# Backing up your customizations

After completing this chapter and customizing all of your nodes, groups, and applications; it is recommended to back everything up. This section will explain the procedure for creating a backup file that you can use for disaster recovery:

1. Log in to the Orion web console.

2. Navigate to **Orion Website Administration** by clicking on **Settings**.

3. Click on **Manage Custom Properties** under **Node & Group Management**.

4. Select **[No Grouping]** from the **Group by:** drop-down menu.

5. Sort by **Object** by clicking on it.

6. Select all **Nodes** by checking the box next to each node **Property Name**.

7. Click on **Export Values** in the toolbar.

8. Select all **columns** in the **Export Custom Properties** page, and choose your preferred file type (for example, * . csv).

9. Click the **Export** button and click **Save** to choose your preferred file location.

 If necessary, repeat this procedure and modify step 6 to select **Interface** property names.

# Summary

After completing this chapter you should be trained to thoroughly tailor SolarWinds SAM to your organization's network environment. Depending on the size of the company it can be a tedious initial process, but the end result will be well worth it.

Next we will explore advanced features, including events, SNMP traps, and alerts. These features will be more beneficial if you methodically customize SolarWinds SAM beforehand.

In this chapter, we covered how to:

- Manually add nodes, VMHosts, and applications
- Automatically add nodes and applications via network scanning
- Remove and disable nodes and applications
- Promote nodes
- Classify nodes with company-specific custom properties
- Create groups and populate them with nodes
- Assign network infrastructure dependencies
- Backup customizations

# 4
# Events, Traps, and Alerts

After SolarWinds SAM deployment, configuration, and customization, we can begin utilizing its advanced features. This chapter will explain how to review events, set traps, and configure alerts. A basic SolarWinds SAM deployment is still useful; however, we recommend that you make use of these advanced elements, as they are particularly beneficial to help in guaranteeing high availability of the IT services.

 Descriptions and procedures in this chapter assume your **HomeTab** toolbar is set as **Admin**. This is the default setting, found under **Settings | Manage Accounts**, and covered in the *Active Directory integration* section of *Chapter 2, Installing and Configuring SolarWinds SAM*.

## Reviewing events

There are various areas within the Orion web console to review events. Event types described in this section are accessible through the **Orion Summary Home** page as concise quick look snap-ins.

The **Message Center** is the centralized location for events, triggered alerts, syslog messages, and received traps, all covered later in this chapter and in *Chapter 5, Syslog, Reporting, and Network Atlas*.

To access all SolarWinds SAM event types, navigate to the **Message Center** by selecting it in the **HomeTab** toolbar. You can also select **Events** directly, or click on **Event Summary**.

| HOME | APPLICATIONS | VIRTUALIZATION | | | | | | | |
|---|---|---|---|---|---|---|---|---|---|
| Summary | Groups | Top 10 | Events | Alerts | Syslog | Traps | Message Center | Reports | Event Summary |

The event types within SolarWinds SAM are as follows:

- **Events**: This tab is a consolidated version of polling information from all nodes that were imported into SolarWinds SAM. Event examples include a node failing and losing connectivity (for example, a catastrophic event), a node experiencing packet loss, or a volume reaching capacity. Events also list significant node modifications such as adding or removing nodes. The following screenshot displays a series of events during an outage, and shows why it is advantageous to label nodes, as the default node named **192.168.1.22** is not informative:

- **Audit Events**: This snap-in is displayed on Orion home page and contains a list of all modifications made to SolarWinds SAM. Examples include changing the name of a node, creating or assigning custom properties, or creating a group.

- **Event Summary**: This tab displays a condensed version of events, sorted by type, and is used as a quick reference to overview recent events. Selecting a category will drill down to specific events that occurred.

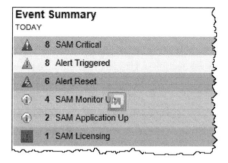

# Adjusting events log retention

By default SolarWinds SAM only retains events for 30 days. If storage capacity is not a problem, you can adjust the retention period dating back further than 30 days. Also, if space is an issue, you may also want to consider a 10-day retention period.

The following procedure explains how to adjust the number of days SolarWinds SAM retains event logs:

1. Log in to the Orion web console.
2. Navigate to Orion Website Administration by clicking on Settings.
3. Click on Polling Settings.
4. Under **Database Settings** you can change **Events Retention** from **30 Days** to something appropriate for your environment.

# Utilizing SNMP traps

SNMP traps are beneficial for choosing a specific node event type, and then consolidating it within the **Traps** page of the Orion web console and the Orion Trap Viewer application. SNMP traps authorize nodes to send specified events immediately when they occur without waiting for SolarWinds SAM to reach out and poll the node. This can help save bandwidth and ensure that SolarWinds SAM is not flooded with uninformative information.

This section will cover the basic mechanisms behind SNMP and how to empower Windows servers and Cisco devices to utilize SNMP traps, and will conclude with examples of how to test and then review triggered traps.

# Understanding SNMP functionality

SNMP exchanges messages between SolarWinds SAM and SNMP enabled nodes. The various message types are explained as follows:

- GET and GET-NEXT: This permits SolarWinds SAM to request a specific variable (that is, information) from a node.

- SET: This permits SolarWinds SAM to request a change to the value of a specific variable from a node.

- RESPONSE: Upon receiving a GET, GET-NEXT, or SET message, a node will issue a RESPONSE message to SolarWinds SAM, containing error reporting fields.

- TRAP: This permits a node to inform SolarWinds SAM of a specified event, by means of an unsolicited message. This is the only SNMP message capable of being initiated by a node. It is intended to notify SolarWinds SAM as soon as an important event occurs.

Information is passed along in the form of data objects contained within a **Management Information Base (MIB)**. MIBs are text files that contain hierarchically organized data objects. Each object has a unique **Object Identifier (OID)** attached to it.

This is important to understand because SolarWinds SAM receives SNMP trap information by referencing OIDs contained within MIBs.

SNMP, WMI, or ICMP can be used to poll a node configured to send SNMP traps. This means it is not mandatory to poll a node with SNMP for SolarWinds SAM to receive SNMP trap information. SolarWinds SAM does not even need to be polling a node for it to receive SNMP trap information. This is where the bandwidth saving benefits can come in to play. With that said, demoting nodes is recommended, as opposed to deleting nodes from SolarWinds SAM.

# Setting SNMP traps on Windows

Windows sends SNMP traps by means of extracting and converting Windows events that were logged in the **Event Viewer**. To utilize Windows SNMP traps you must first enable and configure the **SNMP Service** and the **SNMP Trap** service. After configuring these services you must run the `evntwin.exe` utility to convert Windows events into SNMP traps.

The following are the three procedures that are listed in this section:

- How to enable the SNMP Trap service
- How to configure the SNMP Service to communicate with SolarWinds SAM
- How to set traps in Windows via the `evntwin.exe` utility

Procedures in this section apply to Windows Server 2008 R2 and with minor modifications will translate well to other versions.

# Enabling a Windows SNMP Trap service

The SNMP Trap service description can be misleading, as it implies that it is designed exclusively for receiving traps. However, it must also be enabled for Windows to send traps to SolarWinds SAM.

This procedure explains how to start the SNMP Trap service on a Windows server, and ensure that it automatically starts on reboot.

By default, Windows SNMP Trap service is stopped.

1. Log in to a Windows server.
2. Navigate to **Start Menu | Control Panel | Administrative Tools | Services**.
3. Double-click on the **SNMP Trap** service.
4. On the **General** tab, change **Startup type** to **Automatic**.
5. Click on the **Apply** button.
6. Under **Service status** click on the **Start** button.

# Configuring a Windows SNMP Service for traps

The following procedure outlines how to configure Windows SNMP Service to send traps to SolarWinds SAM:

1. Log in to a Windows server.
2. Navigate to **Start Menu | Control Panel | Administrative Tools | Services**.
3. Double-click on **SNMP Service**.
4. Select the **Traps** tab.
5. Under **Community name**, enter an appropriate name to identify the server. For example, we used Domain Controller 1.

 Do not confuse **Trap** tab's **Community name** of Windows SNMP Service (in step 5) with the **Security** tab's **Community Name** (explained in the *Enabling and configuring SNMP on Windows* section of *Chapter1, Deployment Strategy*). The **Traps** tab's **Community name** is used to label received traps; it is essentially a friendly name.

An example will be provided later in the *Testing and reviewing SNMP traps* section of this chapter.

6. Click on the **Add to list** button.
7. Click on the **Add** button under **Trap destinations**.
8. Type the **Hostname** or **IP Address** of the SolarWinds SAM server. For example, we used jabba.greenbrierlab.com.

9. Click on **OK**.

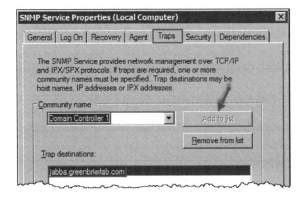

Keep in mind that the SNMP Service's **Security** tab does not need to be configured for a Windows server to send SNMP traps to SolarWinds SAM.

# Converting Windows events into SNMP traps

The following procedure explains how to set SNMP traps on a Windows server by leveraging **Windows Event Viewer** messages via the **Event to Trap Translator** (evntwin.exe) utility.

The **Event to Trap Translator** utility lists all Windows event types and allows them to be translated to traps. There is a large list of event types to choose from. A good starting point is to open Windows Event Viewer, review recent and past events, and then take note of event IDs that may be advantageous to trap.

1. Log in to a Windows server.
2. Click on the Start menu and in **Search programs and files** type evntwin.exe to open the **Event to Trap Translator** utility.

If Windows could not find evntwin.exe then try opening it from the **Command Prompt** by typing cmd in **Search programs and files**.

From **Command Prompt** type the following commands:

`C:\Users\username>cd\`

`C:\>cd win*\sys*32`

`C:\Windows\System32>evntwin.exe`

3. Click on **Yes** if a **User Account Control** window appears.

4. Choose **Custom** under the **Configuration** panel.

5. From the **Event to Trap Translator** utility window click on the **Edit >>** button to display the **Event sources** and **Events** panes.

6. Select the **Events** that you would like to trap and click on the **Add** button.

7. By double-clicking on an **Event** you can open its **Properties** to adjust the **Generate trap** criteria. The settings available are **Count** and **Time**. See the screenshot at the end of this procedure for a practical example.

8. You can adjust settings for all selected SNMP traps by clicking on the **Settings** button. The default settings will normally suffice.

9. Once finished adding and configuring traps, click on **Apply** then **OK**.

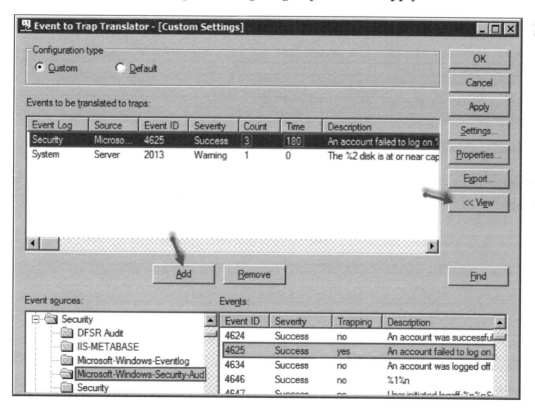

Two SNMP traps were set in the preceding screenshot, described here:

- Under the **Event sources** pane, navigate to **Security | Microsoft-Windows-Security-Auditing** labeled with a **Event ID** of **4625**; this will trap an event when someone attempts to log in to Windows server with bad credentials. To prevent from trapping unnecessary information, we set the **Count** to 3 and **Time** to 180 seconds. This will ensure the event is only trapped on three failed logon attempts within a three minute timeframe, and will prevent from trapping most common password typos. We will refer to this later as the **failed DC1 logon attempts trap**.

- Under the **Event sources** pane, navigate to **System | Server** labeled as **Event ID** of **2013**; this will trap an event when a hard disk drive is nearing or at capacity. The default is 10 percent hard drive space remaining.

# Setting SNMP traps on Cisco devices

The following procedure explains how to enable and configure SNMP traps on a Cisco Catalyst 3550 switch running IOS version 12.1(20)EA1a. In this example, we will explain how to set a trap to notify SolarWinds SAM whenever a command is issued to the switch.

Your network switch types may vary, and have a different set of information to trap. In addition, routers, firewalls, and other various network devices need to be taken into consideration. You will need to research different SNMP traps per device, by consulting the manufacture's website or manual.

1. **Telnet** to the switch (replace `192.168.1.230` with your switch IP):

   ```
   C:\>telnet 192.168.1.230
   ```

2. Type `enable` at the prompt and enter the **enable password**:

   ```
   3550>enable
   Password:
   3550#
   ```

3. Type `configure terminal` at the prompt:

   ```
   3550#configure terminal
   3550(config)#
   ```

4. Issue the `snmp-server enable traps` command:

   ```
   3550(config)#snmp-server enable traps config
   ```

In this command, `config` is used after `enable traps` to designate the trap type. We will refer to this later as the **Cisco3550 config trap**.

5. Appoint SolarWinds SAM as the host networking monitoring service:

```
3550(config)#snmp-server host 192.168.1.3 version 2c
S4MCisco3550SW1
```

In this command, `version 2c` designates SNMPv2C. `S4MCisco3550S1` designates the SNMP community string, and `192.168.1.3` is the IP of our SolarWinds SAM server.

6. Exit the configuration terminal to save your changes, and then verify the new community string:

```
3550(config)#exit
```

```
3550#show running-configuration
```

To remove an SNMP trap or the specified host network monitoring service (that is, SolarWinds SAM), insert a `no` in front of the command issued in step 4 or 5. This will be necessary if you made a typo.

# Testing and reviewing SNMP traps

Each SNMP trap that is set should be tested to ensure the trap is working. Testing traps will also give you an opportunity to familiarize yourself with the **Traps** page within the Orion web console, or within the standalone Orion Trap Viewer application.

Remember to be cautious when testing certain types of SNMP traps, such as a trap on a switch that triggers when a **Virtual LAN (VLAN)** is modified. Testing traps that could bring services down should be performed during non-business hours, or on non-production devices.

This section contains two procedures:

- How to test and review SNMP traps via the Orion web console
- How to test and review SNMP traps via the Orion Trap Viewer

Examples will explain how to test the failed DC1 logon attempts trap and the Cisco3550 config trap examples from the above-mentioned procedures.

> The SNMP trap retention default in SolarWinds SAM is 7 days. Use the procedures mentioned in the *Adjusting events log retention* section of this chapter and modify step 4 by adjusting **Trap Messages Retention**.

# Reviewing SNMP traps in the Orion web console

The following procedure explains how to test and then review SNMP traps within the Orion web console.

First, test a trap; for example, we will use our failed DC1 logon attempts trap.

1.  Click on the Start menu and type `mstsc` in **Search programs and files**.

2.  From the **Remote Desktop Connection** utility enter the server where the failed DC1 logon attempts trap was set. For example, we used our DC `192.168.1.10`.

3.  At the login screen, enter bad credentials 3 times to trigger the trap.

Second, review the trap output received by SolarWinds SAM.

1.  Log in to the Orion web console.

2.  Navigate to logs of received SNMP traps by clicking on **Traps**, or **Message Center**, in the **HomeTab** toolbar. This procedure references going directly to the **Traps** page.

If everything was configured properly, then the triggered trap will be displayed and populated with the following information:

*   **TIME OF TRAP**: This is the timestamp of when the trap was received.

*   **IP ADDRESS**: This is the IP address of the node where the trap originated. For example, in the following screenshot, **192.168.1.10** is the IP address of our domain controller.

*   **HOSTNAME**: This is the hostname of the node where the trap originated. For example, in the following screenshot, **excalibur.greenbrierlab.com** is the hostname of our domain controller.

- **COMMUNITY**: This is the community string assigned to the node where the trap originated. For example, in the following screenshot, **Domain Controller 1** is the friendly trap community name assigned to our domain controller.

- **TRAP TYPE**: This is the MIB and OID information of the trap itself. The OID is the long series of numbers separated by decimal points. For example, in the following screenshot, **35** is the beginning of the OID for our failed DC1 logon attempts trap.

- **TRAP DETAILS**: This is where the trap insertion strings are displayed. Certain trap details can be verbose and complicated. This is one reason why it is a good idea to test each trap and become familiar with each traps output. For example, in the following screenshot, **eventVar9 = Unknown user name or bad password** indicates that this was our failed DC1 logon attempts trap.

 For the sake of this example, in the following screenshot we cropped off most of the OID, as they can be quite long.

| COMMUNITY | TRAP TYPE | TRAP DETAILS |
|---|---|---|
| | | snmpTrapEnterprise = EVENT-LOG-TRAP-MIB:eventLogMib.35.77.105.99.114.111.115.111.102.116.45.87.105.110.100.111.119.115.45.83.101.99.117.114.105.116.121.45.65.117.100.105.116.105.110.103 |
| | | experimental.1057.1.0 = 192.168.1.10 |
| | | sysUpTime = 1 hour 12 minutes 19.78 seconds |
| | | snmpTrapOID = EVENT-LOG-TRAP-MIB:eventLogMib.35.77.105.99.114.111.115.111.102.116.45.87.105.110.100.111.119.115.45.83.101.99.117.114.105.116.121.45.65.117.100.105.116.105.110.103.0.4625 |
| | | eventLogMibObjects.26.0 = - |
| | | eventLogMibObjects.25.0 = - |
| | | eventLogMibObjects.24.0 = - |
| | | eventLogMibObjects.23.0 = 0x0 |
| | | eventLogMibObjects.22.0 = 0 |
| | | eventLogMibObjects.21.0 = - |
| | | eventVar15 = - |
| | | eventVar14 = JCOMP |
| | | eventVar13 = NTLM |
| | | eventVar12 = NtLmSsp |
| | | eventVar11 = 3 |
| | | eventVar10 = 0xc0000064 |
| Domain Controller 1 | EVENT-LOG-TRAP-MIB:eventLogMib.35.77.105.99.114.111.115.111.102.116.45.87.105.110.100.111.119.115.45 | eventVar9 = Unknown user name or bad password. |
| | | eventVar8 = 0xc000006d |
| | | eventVar7 = GREENBRIERLAB |
| | | eventVar6 = EviLHaCkEr |
| | | eventVar5 = S-1-0-0 |
| | | eventVar4 = 0x0 |

# Reviewing SNMP traps in the Orion Trap Viewer

Orion Trap Viewer is a standalone application designed to display triggered SNMP traps. It also includes added functionality by allowing the creation of rules.

 Orion Trap Viewer application is included with SolarWinds SAM.

First, test a trap; for example, we will use our Cisco3550 config trap.

1.  Telnet to the switch (replace `192.168.1.230` with your switch IP):

    ```
    C:\>telnet 192.168.1.230
    ```

2.  Type `enable` at the prompt and enter the enable password:

    ```
    3550>enable
    Password:
    3550#
    ```

3.  Issue a non-intrusive command to **trigger the trap**:

    ```
    3550#show running-config
    ```

Second, review the trap output received by SolarWinds SAM.

1.  Launch Orion Trap Viewer by navigating to **Start | All Programs | Syslog and SNMP Traps | Trap Viewer**.

2.  The output of our Cisco3550 config trap is displayed in the following screenshot. The fields described in the preceding section will be the same as displayed in the Orion web console's **Traps** page.

| Trap Time | IP | Hostname | Community | Trap Type | Trap Details |
|---|---|---|---|---|---|
| 8/1/2013 9:42:57 PM | 192.168.1.230 | 192.168.1.230 | S4MCisco3550SW1 | CISCO-CONFIG-MAN-MIB:cisco ConfigManEvent | sysUpTime=7 days 0 hours 30 minutes 20.52 seconds snmpTrapOID=CISCO-CONFIG-MAN-MIB:ciscoConfigManEvent ccmHistoryEventCommandSource.93=commandLine(1) ccmHistoryEventConfigSource.93=3 ccmHistoryEventConfigDestination.93=2 |

From Orion Trap Viewer, SNMP traps can be refined and filtered via rules created by navigating to **Edit | Add Rule**, or by right-clicking on a trap and selecting **Add Rule**. Each tab within the **Add Rule** window includes the trap fields (that is, **Trap Time**, **IP**, **Trap Details**, and so on). Comparison criteria can be modified for each field by changing the default wildcard * to regular expressions used for pattern matching. From within a rule you can also apply an e-mail alert to notify you via e-mail if an SNMP trap is triggered.

 Procedures and examples for creating Trap rules are referenced on the author's blog: http://justinmbrant.blogspot.com/.

# Managing alerts

Effective alerting is contingent on diligently configuring and customizing applicable nodes. By default, alerting is preconfigured by SolarWinds SAM in a logical and useful manner. All that is really necessary for effective alerting is to forward suitable alerts to e-mail, and make minor alterations to designated alerts.

Procedures in this section explain how to review alerts and point alerts to e-mail by using the Orion web console, and Advanced Alert Manager application.

# Reviewing and modifying alerts

All triggered alerts will be logged and displayed in the Orion web console under **Alerts**, accessible from the **HomeTab** toolbar. As with **Events**, **Traps**, and **Syslog**, **Alerts** can also be accessed via the **Message Center** tab.

**Alerts** will appear as unacknowledged, or can be flagged **Acknowledged** by checking the box next to them, then clicking on the **Acknowledge Alerts** button. This is one reason to complete the procedures mentioned in the *Active Directory integration* section of *Chapter 2, Installing and Configuring SolarWinds SAM*, since the approver's username will be listed under the **ACKNOWLEDGED BY** field. This is beneficial as a supplementary process in a change management **standard operating procedure (SOP)**.

For example, in the following screenshot, acknowledged alerts are labeled as **jbrant** in the **ACKNOWLEDGED BY** field; in addition, this is another example of why it is important to thoroughly label your nodes, as the default node named **192.168.1.15** is uninformative.

| | | TIME OF ALERT | ALERT NAME | ALERT TYPE | NETWORK OBJECT | ACKNOWLEDGED BY | ACKNOWLEDGED TIME |
|---|---|---|---|---|---|---|---|
| ☐ | ⚠ | 8/2/2013 9:45 AM | Alert me when a node goes down | Advanced | Cisco 3550 Switch 1 | | |
| ☐ | ⚠ | 8/2/2013 9:44 AM | High Packet Loss Monitoring | Advanced | Cisco 3550 Switch 1 | | |
| ☐ | ⚠ | 8/2/2013 5:57 AM | Alert me when a node goes down | Advanced | vguinevere.greenbrierlab.com | | |
| ☐ | ⚠ | 8/2/2013 5:56 AM | High Packet Loss Monitoring | Advanced | vguinevere.greenbrierlab.com | | |
| ☑ | ⚠ | 7/28/2013 12:58 PM | Alert me when a node goes down | Advanced | 192.168.1.15 | GREENBRIERLAB\jbrant Orion Website | 8/2/2013 1:49:15 PM |
| | ⚠ | 7/28/2013 | High Packet Loss | Advanced | | GREENBRIERLAB\jbrant | 8/2/2013 1:49:15 |

> Types of alerts received can be set by navigating to **Settings** | **Manage Advanced Alerts**.

# Forwarding alerts via e-mail

Automated alerting to e-mail is perhaps the most useful feature in SolarWinds SAM. After SolarWinds SAM is thoroughly configured, e-mail alerts can be one of the most valuable IT tools to ensure service levels are met.

The following procedure will explain how to utilize **Advanced Alert Manager** application to alert you via e-mail when a node goes down.

> We recommend using a distribution list or a group e-mail inbox for alerts.

1. Launch Advanced Alert Manager by navigating to **Start** | **All Programs** | **Alerting, Reporting and Mapping** | **Advanced Alert Manager**.
2. Click on the **Configure Alerts** button.
3. Select **Alert me when a node goes down** and click on the **Edit** button.
4. From the **General** tab, ensure that **Enable this Alert** is checked.

5. Select the **Trigger Actions** tab and click on the **Add New Action** button.

6. Select **Send an E-Mail/Page** and click on **OK**.

7. Enter an e-mail address in the **To, CC,** and/or **BCC** fields.

8. Select the **SMTP Server** tab and enter appropriate data in the **hostname** or **IP Address** field of your SMTP server. Select **Enable SSL** and/or **SMTP authentication** if necessary.

9. Select the **Time of Day** tab if you wish to apply a custom schedule.

10. Select the **Alert Escalation** tab and consider if enabling **Execute this Action repeatedly while the Alert is triggered** makes sense for your environment. This setting is useful to prevent a flood of e-mail alerts.

11. Test the e-mail alert by rebooting a node that is not vital to IT services.

 We recommend browsing through all preconfigured alerts in the **Manage Alerts** window and repeating this procedure to enable a variety of e-mail alerts.

 Procedures and examples for creating custom alerts are referenced on the author's blog: `http://justinmbrant.blogspot.com/`.

# Summary

After completing this chapter we have acquired hands on experience in some of the advanced functionality included with SolarWinds SAM. Next, we will cover additional advanced features, including syslog, reporting, and Orion Network Atlas.

In this chapter, we learned how to:

- Review events and adjust the retention period
- Utilize SNMP traps on Windows servers
- Utilize SNMP traps on Cisco devices
- Test and review SNMP traps in SolarWinds SAM
- Manage advanced alerts
- Simulate and test alerts

# 5

# Syslog, Reporting, and Network Atlas

This chapter will cover an overview of the Syslog, how to configure and run reports, and then explain **Orion Network Atlas**. These advanced features will ensure that you get the most out of your SolarWinds SAM deployment.

## Utilizing Syslog

The Syslog messages are stored on nodes and can be forwarded to SolarWinds SAM as the centralized repository. As with polling and SNMP traps, each node must be configured accordingly. Administrators should research available Syslog information per node, then break it down to a granular level and decide which log data should be forwarded to SolarWinds SAM. Small to mid-sized organizations may decide to forward most (if not all) Syslog information, whereas larger enterprises will need to plan methodically due to volume constraints and database stability.

Procedures in this section will cover an overview of Syslog, and ensure that the log data is transferred to SolarWinds SAM by enabling and configuring Syslog forwarding on some common Cisco devices. We will conclude the section with an example of testing the procedures in order to review Syslog data within Orion web console and the standalone **Syslog Viewer** application.

 Similarly to SNMP Traps, Windows events can be converted to Syslog messages and forwarded to SolarWinds SAM; Syslog functionality is not integrated within Windows. Therefore, this book will not include a procedure to accomplish this. Tutorials for utilizing the Syslog on Windows can be found on the author's blog: http://justinmbrant.blogspot.com

# Understanding Syslog

Syslog is a standard for data logging, most commonly used on network devices, relevant applications (for example, IIS, Exchange), and Linux. Each Syslog message is often labeled with the fields. Syslog fields are not standardized, and they are dependent on implementation and configuration.

The following are the Syslog fields:

- **Facility**: This field has a numerically assigned value **0** through **23** which is used for providing a rough clue to indicate the part of a node, about where the message originated from.

  The author's blog includes facility code definitions:
  `http://justinmbrant.blogspot.com`

- **Severity**: This field has a numerically assigned value indicating the severity of the message; 0 being the most severe and 7 being the least severe.
    - **Level 0 (Emergency)**: This indicates that the system is unstable; a panic condition (that is, a catastrophic event)
    - **Level 1 (Alert)**: This indicates the loss of a primary system and to take action immediately
    - **Level 2 (Critical)**: This indicates a failure of a secondary system and to take action promptly
    - **Level 3 (Error)**: This is a non-urgent failure, indicating a critical event may occur if unaddressed
    - **Level 4 (Warning)**: This condition indicates that an error may occur if unaddressed
    - **Level 5 (Notice)**: This is normally used to spot potential problems before they occur
    - **Level 6 (Informational)**: This is generally used for reporting and metrics
    - **Level 7 (Debug)**: This occurs only during debugging and is normally used by developers

When forwarding Syslog messages by severity, the lowest severity level chosen will include all greater severity levels. For example, when choosing severity level 3 (Error) it will also encompass severity levels: 2 (Critical), 1 (Alert), and 0 (Emergency).

Commonly, organizations only send messages with a severity of 0 through 3 to SolarWinds SAM.

- **Timestamp**: This field indicates the date and time that the message was initiated.

- **Host**: This field indicates the IP address of the node that initiated the message.

Be aware each Syslog message has a 1 KB limitation and is not considered the most secure or reliable protocol. As mentioned, the message format is not standardized; therefore, at times it may be difficult or confusing to decipherer.

# Forwarding Syslog on common Cisco devices

Procedures within this section provide examples of how to forward Syslog data to SolarWinds SAM from some common Cisco devices. The first procedure is performed on a Cisco ASA 5505 firewall, by using the **Adaptive Security Device Manager** (**ASDM**) application. Firewalls gather a great deal of useful information regarding network activity; therefore, harvesting Syslog data from these devices is practical and advantageous. The subsequent procedure will explain how to send Syslog data from a Cisco Catalyst 3550 switch to SolarWinds SAM.

## Enabling and configuring Syslog forwarding on Cisco firewall

The following procedure will explain how to enable and configure a Cisco ASA 5505 firewall to forward all Syslog data with a severity of 0 through 3 to SolarWinds SAM:

1. Run the ASDM Java application by typing the IP address (use `https`) of the ASA into the web browser and click on **Run ASDM**. For example, we use `https://192.168.1.254`.

2. Enter the administrator credentials.

3. Click on the **Configuration** tab in the toolbar.

4. Select **Device Management** in the bottom-left pane.

5. Select **Logging** in the **Device Management** pane.

6. Select **Syslog Servers** from **Logging**.

7. Click on the **Add** button in the upper-right corner of the ASDM.

8. From the **Add Syslog Server** window:

   1. If SolarWinds SAM lives on the same subnet as the ASDM, then for **Interface** select **inside**. If it resides on another subnet use **outside**.

   2. Type the **IP Address** of the SolarWinds SAM server. For example, we use `192.168.1.3`.

   3. Select **Protocol: UDP** and leave the default port as **514** and click on **OK**. By default, SolarWinds SAM listens for Syslog messages on **UDP** port **514**.

9. Click on **Apply**.

10. Make sure to click on **Save** in the toolbar.

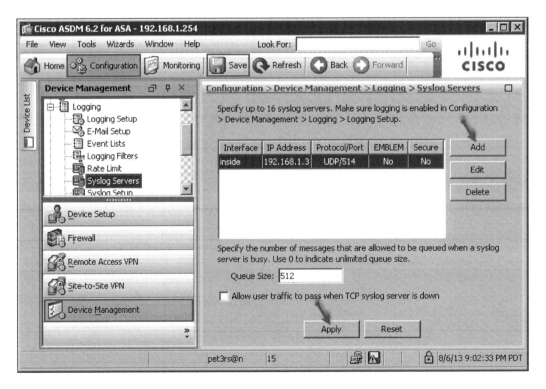

11. Select **Logging Filters** from **Logging**.

12. Double-click on **Syslog Servers** from the right pane.

13. From the **Edit Logging Filters** window under **Syslogs from All Event Classes**, click on **Filter on severity** then use the drop-down menu to select **Errors**. This will ensure all Syslog messages between severity 0 and 3 will be forwarded to SolarWinds SAM.

> Within the **Event Logging Filters** window, forwarded Syslog messages can be further refined per each facility and severity, by using the **Syslogs from Specific Event Class**. Advanced procedures for refining Cisco ASA Syslog forwarding are included on the author's blog: `http://justinmbrant.blogspot.com`

14. Click on **OK**.

15. Click on **Apply** and make sure to click on **Save** in the toolbar.

# Enabling and configuring Syslog forwarding on a Cisco switch

The following procedure explains how to enable and configure a Cisco Catalyst 3550 switch running IOS version 12.1(20)EA1a for forwarding Syslog messages with severity of 0 through 3 to SolarWinds SAM:

1. Telnet to the switch (replace `192.168.1.230` with your switch IP):

   ```
   C:\>telnet 192.168.1.230
   ```

2. Type `enable` at the prompt and enter the enable password:

   ```
   3550>enable
   Password:
   3550#
   ```

3. Type `configure terminal` at the prompt:

   ```
   3550#configure terminal
   Enter configuration commands, one per line.  End with CNTL/Z.
   3550(config)#
   ```

4. Assign SolarWinds SAM as the Syslog server. For example, we use `192.168.1.3`.

   ```
   3550(config)#logging 192.168.1.3
   ```

5. Tell the switch to forward all Syslog messages:

```
3550(config)#facility syslog
```

6. Tell the switch to only forward messages with a severity between 0 and 3:

```
3550(config)#logging trap 3
```

> In the preceding command, choosing 3 represents `error` and will forward all Syslog data between severity level 0 (Emergency) through 3 (Error).

7. Exit the configuration terminal, save your changes, and then verify the Syslog forwarding configuration:

```
3550(config)#exit
3550#
3550#wr
3550#show running-configuration
```

# Testing and reviewing Syslog data in SolarWinds SAM

To ensure SolarWinds SAM is receiving Syslog data, Syslog forwarding should be tested (as with SNMP traps) in a risk-free manner. We will test both Syslog procedures described previously, simply by modifying one step to forward severity level 5 (Notifications) and up.

- To test the Cisco ASA firewall Syslog forwarding procedure, modify step 13 and change **Errors** to **Notifications** within the drop-down menu.

- To test the Cisco 3550 switch Syslog forwarding procedure, modify step 6 and change `trap 3` to `trap 5`.

> After this test, change these settings back to severity level 3 (Error).

After lowering the severity level criteria, wait a few minutes and, if everything was configured properly, then you should see the **Notification** events populating within Orion web console and within **Syslog Viewer** application. This procedure will explain how to review the SolarWinds SAM Syslog.

1. Log in to the Orion web console.

2. From the **Orion Summary Home** tab within the Orion web console select **Syslog** from the toolbar, or select the **Message Center**.

| HOME | APPLICATIONS | VIRTUALIZATION |
| --- | --- | --- |

Summary   Groups   Top 10   Events   Alerts   Syslog   Traps   Message Center   Reports   Event Summary

3. Syslog messages sent from configured nodes will be displayed on this page, sorted by timestamp, and color coordinated by severity level. For example, in the following screenshot, the message with severity level **Error** is labeled red. The screenshot also shows that the Cisco ASA firewall **192.168.1.254** immediately starts sending notification messages after changing the severity level to 5 (Notification).

To quickly confirm the Cisco Catalyst 3550 switch **192.168.1.230** was sending messages, we logged into it and issued a `show running-configuration` command. This sends a notification message labeled **Confirmed from console by vty0**, as displayed in the following screenshot.

The screenshot also shows that the Cisco ASA firewall **192.168.1.254** immediately starts sending notification messages after changing the severity level to 5 (Notification).

| | TIME OF MESSAGE | HOSTNAME | SEVERITY | MESSAGE |
| --- | --- | --- | --- | --- |
| ☐ | 8/8/2013 7:10:41 PM | 192.168.1.254 | Notice | %ASA-5-713120: Group = 64.87.27.74, IP = 64.87.27.74, PHASE 2 COMPLETED (msgid=c7aaeb72) |
| ☐ | 8/8/2013 7:10:40 PM | 192.168.1.254 | Error | %ASA-3-713122: IP = 64.87.27.74, Keep-alives configured on but peer does not support keep-alives |
| ☐ | 8/8/2013 7:10:40 PM | 192.168.1.254 | Notice | %ASA-5-713119: Group = 64.87.27.74, IP = 64.87.27.74, PHASE 1 COMPLETED |
| ☐ | 8/8/2013 7:10:40 PM | 192.168.1.254 | Warning | %ASA-4-713903: Group = 64.87.27.74, IP = 64.87.27.74, Freeing previously allocated memory for au |
| ☐ | 8/8/2013 7:09:07 PM | 192.168.1.230 | Notice | 20: 05:19:53: Configured from console by vty0 (192.168.1.3) |
| ☐ | 8/8/2013 6:57:41 PM | 192.168.1.254 | Notice | %ASA-5-111008: User 'jbranf' executed the 'dir disk0:/dap.xml' command. |

You can also view received Syslog messages from **Syslog Viewer** application, by navigating to **Start Menu | SolarWinds Orion | Syslog Viewer**.

This standalone application displays the same Syslog messages as the Orion web console, but also has added functionality by allowing the creation of **Syslog Rules** and **Custom Syslog Alerts**. Advanced tutorials on these features are included on the author's blog: http://justinmbrant.blogspot.com

# Utilizing reporting

Reporting is beneficial for reviewing recent and historical data that SolarWinds SAM has collected, ranging from a broad to a granular level. A set of convenient predefined reports are included for out of the box reporting. Predefined report types include: **Application Reports, Group Reports, Hardware Health Reports, Interface Reports**, and **Node Reports**. Each predefined report type contains a number of individual reports that will provide a specific output. Most reports will only apply to nodes configured to be polled by SNMP or WMI.

Each SolarWinds SAM predefined report is labeled and described intuitively within Orion web console; therefore, a detailed explanation for each report will not be included in this book. We recommend that you browse through each predefined report and familiarize yourself with its intended purpose.

SolarWinds SAM also includes a **Report Writer** application, which can be used to create new reports, or modify pre-existing reports. SolarWinds SAM also includes Orion Report Scheduler, which is used to schedule report jobs, and Orion Report Writer, which is used to create and modify reports. These are both standalone applications.

Procedures within this section outline how to:

- Run and review the predefined reports within Orion web console.
- Create a report with Orion Report Writer.
- Schedule a report via Orion Report Scheduler.

# Running reports

This procedure explains how to run and review a predefined report from within the Orion web console, specifically, a report designed to **Display the Average CPU Load for all Nodes Last Month**.

1. Log in to the Orion web console.

2. From the **Orion Summary Home** page select **Reports**.

3. Scroll to **Node Reports** and expand **Historical CPU and Memory Reports**.

4. Click on **CPU Load - Last Month**.

5. As shown in the following screenshot, the output will display the following columns: **Node**, **Vendor**, **Average CPU Load**, and **Peak CPU Load**, for all SNMP and WMI configured nodes. You may sort by column by clicking on the column name. For example, we sort by **Peak CPU Load**.

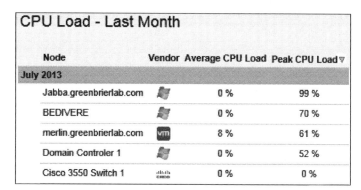

6. It is possible to export or print the report by clicking on the **Export to PDF** or **Printable Version** buttons, located in the upper-right corner of the **Reports** page.

The **Reports** page is one area that is appropriate to grant non-privileged Orion web console access, such as granting access to a Help Desk Technician, who should not have the ability to make changes to SolarWinds SAM, but should be able to review the data it has collected. Procedures for creating Orion web console accounts with varying permissions are covered in the *Active Directory integration* section of *Chapter 2, Installing and Configuring SolarWinds SAM*.

# Creating reports

The standalone Orion Report Writer application allows reports to be created or modified. The following procedure explains how to create a new report for the status of the Network Devices group created in the *Creating groups* section of *Chapter 3, Customizing SolarWinds SAM*.

We will create this report by modifying a predefined report, and then use **Save As**. This is the quickest and easiest method, and you can use it on other predefined reports to create a variety of custom reports for your organization.

1. Log in to the SolarWinds SAM server.

2. Launch Orion Report Writer by navigating to **Start | All Programs | Alerting, Reporting and Mapping | Reports Writer**.

3. Scroll down to **Groups: Current Groups and Group Members Status** and select **Current Status of each Group Member**.

It is easier to view and modify the report if you maximize the window within Orion Report Writer.

4. From the **General** tab, change the **Report Title** field to your new report name and add additional friendly identifiable information, such as the description. You can also change the orientation of the report. For example, we changed the title to Current Status of each Group Member - Network Devices, and make sure that **Make this Report available from the Orion website** is checked.

5. From the **Select Fields** tab, you can review and modify how the report data is listed. We left the default fields. However, for modifying additional predefined reports, it works well to add or remove fields by clicking on the square icon with three periods. An example of this icon is displayed in the following screenshot.

6. From the **Filter Results** tab, refine the data that is pulled from the selected fields by clicking on the square icon with three periods. For example, as displayed in the following screenshot, we performed the following steps, to filter everything except the Network Devices group:

   1. Click on the square icon with three periods and select **Add new elementary condition**.

   2. **Records where * is equal to *** will appear.

   3. Click on the * sign between **where** and **is**.

   4. Navigate to **Group Members | Group | Group Name**.

   5. Click on the * after **equal to**, and type Network Devices.

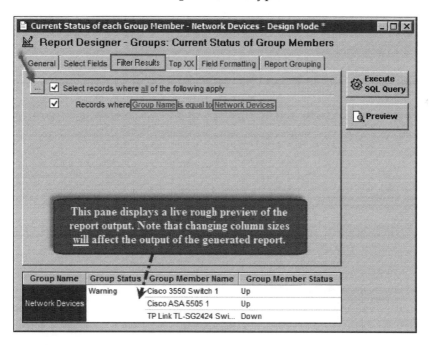

7. The **Top XX** tab is used to scale down reports, which may be too large. For example, you can select **Show only Top X# Records**, or **Show only Top X%  Records**. In this example, we have left the default option, that is, **Show All Records**.

8.  The **Field Formatting** tab allows the field names to be changed. In this example, we have left the default names.

9.  The **Report Grouping** tab allows you to modify how the selected fields are grouped. For example, we click on the **Add New Group** drop-down menu, select **Group_Member_Status**, and click on the **Add Report Group** button. Our report will now group nodes by **Up** or **Down** status.

10. Before saving, test the report output by selecting **Preview** from the toolbar. Return to **Design Mode** by clicking on the **Design** button in the toolbar.

11. From **File**, select **Save As** to ensure that you do not save over the predefined report. For example, we click on **Save As** and name our new report as `Current Status of each Group Member - Network Devices`.

12. The new custom report will now appear and be accessible from Orion web console.

# Scheduling reports

The standalone Orion Report Scheduler application is designed to run, e-mail, and/or print a SolarWinds SAM report at a scheduled interval. In the following procedure, we will create a job that will send an e-mail report that **Displays the Current Space Available for Each Volume** every **Monday** at 8:00 AM:

1.  Log in to the SolarWinds SAM server.

2.  Launch Orion Report Scheduler by navigating to **Start** | **All Programs** | **Alerting, Reporting and Mapping** | **Orion Report Scheduler**.

3.  Click on the **Create a New Job** button.

4.  Type the name for the scheduled report under **Enter a job name**. For example we enter, `All Disk Volumes - Weekly`.

5.  Click on the **Continue** button.

6.  On the **Add a link to a Web Report or Page** window, click on the square icon with three periods to open a window that displays the Orion web console.

    1.  Follow the procedure described in the *Running reports* section of this chapter to browse to a report. Select the report that you would like to schedule and click on the **Use Current URL** button. For example, we navigate to **Node Reports** | **Inventory** | **All Disk Volumes**.

2. Enter the credentials for an account that has permission to view reports within Orion web console. We recommend that you create and use a service account that has the minimum permissions to run SolarWinds SAM reports. For example, we use a service account named SAMReportUser.

3. Click on the **Continue** button.

7. Choose a date and time on the **Select when the job is to be run** window. For example, we:

    1. Select **Weekly** under the **Schedule Job** section.

    2. Enter **Start Time** of 8:00 AM.

    3. Enter **next Monday's date**, under the **Starting On** section.

    4. Leave the **Ending On** field blank.

    5. Enter 1 for **Every week(s) on:** and check the **Monday** checkbox.

    6. Click on the **Continue** button.

8. On the **Select an action to perform** window you can choose to print or e-mail the report as a PDF or HTML. We select **Email the Web Page (as PDF)**. Click on the **Continue** button.

9. On the **Configure the details about the job** window, enter information in the **Email To, Email From**, and **SMTP Server** tab. The following is an explanation and example for each tab:

    1. On the **Email To** tab, enter recipients and a subject line; for example, we enter Network Operations Center (NOC) team distribution list in the **Email Recipients To** field, and All Disk Volumes - Weekly Report for the subject line.

    2. On the **Email From** tab, enter the name and reply address. We use SolarWinds SAM Reports for the name, and donotreply@greenbrierlabs.com for the reply address.

    3. On the **SMTP Server** tab, enter the SMTP hostname or IP address of your SMTP server. For example, we use our Exchange SMTP server IP address of 192.168.1.10.

    4. Click on the **Continue** button.

10. On the **Specify the Windows User Information** window, enter account credentials that will be used to send e-mails. For example, we use the SAMReportUser service account referenced in step 5 of this procedure.

11. Click on the **Continue** button.

12. On the **Add comments about this Job** window, optionally you can add a description about the automated report.

13. Click on the **Finish** button.

14. As displayed in the following screenshot, the job will appear at the top of the **Report Scheduler** window with a checkbox indicating it is enabled. Uncheck the box to disable the job. The job can be edited or deleted by right-clicking on it and selecting **Edit Job** or **Delete Selected Job**.

 You should test the new job by right-clicking on it and selecting **Run Selected Job Now**.

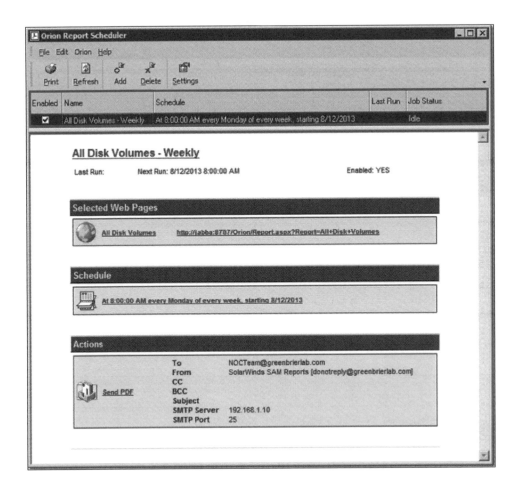

# Orion Network Atlas overview

Included with the SolarWinds SAM bundle is **Orion Network Atlas**, which is designed to create a graphical representation of the geographical layout of networked buildings within an organization. It can also be used to create a network diagram for each location. Maps and diagrams can be printed for the purpose of documentation, and can be connected to the Orion web console, for a live visual depiction of nodes.

All nodes added to SolarWinds SAM can be added to an **Orion Network Atlas** map or diagram. For a diagram you can simply use a blank page and drag nodes onto it, and then connect them accordingly. For a map you can add a background, add nodes to the map, and then connect them accordingly. Thirty three backgrounds of the world and various continents are included, or a map of your own can be used.

# Creating a network map

The following procedure will explain how to use **Orion Network Atlas** to create a network map. Refer to the screenshot at the end of the chapter for an example of the following procedure.

1.  Log in to the SolarWinds SAM server.
2.  Launch **Orion Network Atlas** by navigating to **Start | All Programs | Alerting, Reporting and Mapping | Orion Network Atlas**.

 **Orion Network Atlas** executable can be downloaded from Orion web console and installed on your desktop computer.
`http://localhost:8787/NetworkAtlas/NetworkAtlas.exe`

3.  Log in to the application by entering the credentials used to log in to Orion web console.
4.  By default a background image of the world is added on the right pane, and all SolarWinds SAM nodes and groups are added on the left pane.
5.  Select a background. Click on the **Background** button in the toolbar and select a **Background Image**. All of our organization's buildings are located within the contiguous United States; therefore we selected the `NetworkAtlas_northamerica.jpg` map. Click on **Open**.
6.  Drag nodes from the left pane onto the map. For our example, we place the **Domain Controller SD** node onto San Diego and the **Domain Controller WV** node onto West Virginia.

7.  Select an added node on the map and click on **Select Graphic** from **Options** in the toolbar to assign a graphic to it. We select **Domain Controller SD** and then from within the **Select Graphic Image** window navigate to **Networking Icons | Buildings | medium_building** and click on **OK**. Then scale it down to size. We perform the same process for the **Domain Controller WV** node and assign the **branch_office** graphic to it.

8.  Connect the nodes by clicking on **Straight Line** or **Curved Line** from the toolbar and drag the line from node to node to connect them. You can change the lines appearance in the drop-down menus from within the **Lines** portion of the toolbar. We connected **Domain Controller SD** to **Domain Controller WV** and changed the line type to **Dash**.

> You can also use the **ConnectNow** button under **Topology** in the toolbar to automatically connect nodes.

9.  Add text to your map by clicking on **Add Label** under **Labels** in the toolbar. We add a MPLS label between the sites.

10. Click on the **Save** icon to title your new map. We use Blue Sun Design, LLC.

# Adding network maps to the Orion web console

The following procedure will explain how to add a custom network map to Orion web console, after completing the procedure outlined in the *Creating a network map* section of this chapter:

1.  Log in to the Orion web console.

2.  On the **Orion Summary Home** page you will see a **Sample Application Map** snap-in. Click on the **EDIT** button as shown in the following screenshot.

3.  Change the **Title** of the map from **Sample Application Map**. We use Blue Sun Design, LLC.

4.  Optionally, modify the **Subtitle**. We use www.bluesundesign.net.

5.  Under **Select network map**, select your custom map. We select the **Blue Sun Design, LLC** map designed according to the procedures mentioned in the *Creating a network map* section of this chapter.

6.  Optionally, you can change the **Scale** of the map from **100%**.

7. Click on the **Submit** button.

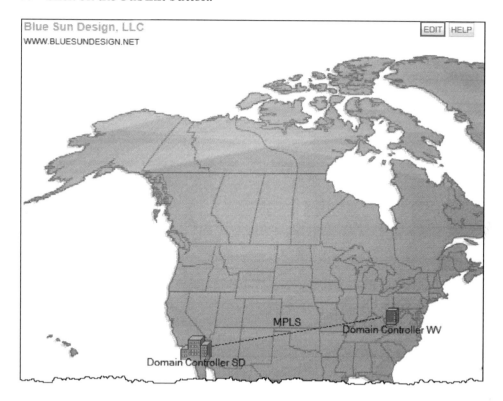

# Summary

By now you should have SolarWinds SAM tailored to the specific needs of your environment and configured as a comprehensive network monitoring service. See *Appendix*, *Troubleshooting*, for troubleshooting tips.

In this chapter, we covered:

- Understanding, forwarding, and testing Syslog messages
- Running, creating, and scheduling reports
- Creating and adding Orion Network Atlas maps and network diagrams

# Troubleshooting

This appendix includes troubleshooting tips to resolve some common issues that may occur during the SolarWinds SAM installation, with the Orion web console, and while attempting to poll nodes with SNMP or WMI. Additional troubleshooting content, applicable to SolarWinds SAM, is posted regularly on the author's blog at http://justinmbrant.blogspot.com.

## Installation issues

You may get an error message during the installation explaining that **Setup is missing an installation prerequisite - Microsoft SQL Server 2012 System CLR**.

To resolve this issue, install both versions of Microsoft® System CLR Types for Microsoft SQL Server 2012 (x86 and x64).

- x86 package:
  http://go.microsoft.com/fwlink/?LinkID=239643&clcid=0x409

- x64 package:
  http://go.microsoft.com/fwlink/?LinkID=239644&clcid=0x409

 If the issue persists, try logging in to the SolarWinds SAM server with a **Local Administrator** account, and then run the installation package.

## Orion web console issues

There are a number of potential issues that may affect the Orion web console. Some common issues and resolutions are listed in this section.

# Problems with IIS

Problems with IIS are commonly system services related. Follow the given procedure to ensure that IIS is installed and running.

1. Log in to the SolarWinds SAM server.

2. Naviagate to **Start** | **Administrative Tools** | **Server Manager** | **Roles** | **Web Server (IIS)**.

3. If IIS is not installed, right-click on **Roles** and select **Add Role**. Follow the **Add Roles Wizard**.

4. If IIS is installed, confirm the required services are running by selecting **Web Server (IIS)** and starting all **System Services** located in the right pane. You should set these services to **Automatically Start** on reboot.

5. If the previous steps didn't work, check **IIS Events** to rule out if IIS is really the cause of the Orion web console issue.

   Go directly to **IIS Events** by selecting **Web Server (IIS)** and click on **Go to Event Viewer** located in the upper-right side of the window. Search for any **Error** or **Warning** events.

# DNS issues

If the Orion web console does not load from a remote machine, then you may have a DNS issue. Follow this procedure to determine if that is the case.

1. Log in to a machine other than the SolarWinds SAM server.

2. Attempt to log in to the Orion web console with the SolarWinds SAM server IP address, for example, `http://192.168.1.3:8787/`.

3. Next, try logging in to the Orion web console with the SolarWinds SAM hostname, for example, `http://jabba:8787/`.

4. If you were successful in logging in with the IP address but not the hostname, then you have a DNS issue. You can either use the IP to connect, or you can work to resolve the DNS issue. You may simply need to add an **A record** to your DNS server.

 The author's blog provides links to tutorials on adding A records on Windows servers; it can be found at `http://justinmbrant.blogspot.com`.

# SolarWinds services

If you receive an error message stating **There was an error communicating with the Orion server** after opening the Orion web console, then you may need to start (or restart) some SolarWinds SAM services.

1.  Log in to the SolarWinds SAM server.
2.  Navigate to **Start | Administrative Tools | Services**.
3.  Browse to the services starting with **SolarWinds**.
4.  Start, or restart, the **SolarWinds Orion Module Engine** service.

 In some instances, this service does not start properly after rebooting the SolarWinds SAM server; this is prior to setting it to **Start Automatically** and to **Restart the Service** after a failure. Manually starting this service will normally resolve the issue, and the service generally remains stable until the next reboot.

5.  Start, or restart, **SolarWinds Service V3**.
6.  Start, or restart, **SolarWinds Service**.
7.  Close the web browser, open it again, and then attempt to log in to the Orion web console.

If the problem persists, you may need to refer to **SolarWinds Knowledge Base** at `http://knowledgebase.solarwinds.com/kb/categories/SolarWinds+Server+%26+Application+Monitor+(SAM,+formerly+APM)/`.

Or, contact SolarWinds support at `http://www.solarwinds.com/support/ticket/`.

# Restarting the Network Sonar Wizard

If the web browser or server crashes while the Network Sonar Wizard (NSW) is running, or you accidently end it prematurely, you can restart it by following the given steps:

1.  Log in to the Orion web console.
2.  Select **Settings** in the upper-right corner of the screen.
3.  Click on **Network Sonar Discovery** under **Getting Started with Orion**.
4.  Select the radio button next to your **Discovery Profile**, normally labeled **admin: <date>, <time>**.
5.  Click on the **Edit** button.
6.  This will take you back to the beginning of NSW.

# SNMP polling issues

Once a community string is assigned, SNMP polling is generally straightforward and worry-free; however, it is possible that issues may still occur. This section is intended to help resolve some common issues.

## Confirming settings

Start by confirming that the SNMP service is enabled and the SNMP community string is set on the node. Then confirm that the SNMP host on the node is referencing the correct IP address or hostname of your SolarWinds SAM server. If you are using the hostname of your SolarWinds SAM server, then try using its IP address to see if that resolves the issue.

After confirming that the node is configured properly, double check the SolarWinds SAM settings and ensure the community string is entered correctly. Remember, the community strings are case sensitive. You should also check that the IP address or hostname is entered correctly as per the node that you are attempting to poll. If you are attempting to poll a node via hostname in SolarWinds SAM, then try using its IP address to see if that resolves the issue.

Refer to SNMP-related procedures in *Chapter 1, Deployment Strategy*, for instructions on how to enable and configure SNMP on nodes. If the node you are trying to poll via SNMP is not listed, then you should refer to the manufacturer's website or its user manual for SNMP configuration procedures.

## The SNMP tab missing on a Windows server

The SNMP tab may be missing if you install the SNMP service on Windows and then immediately try to configure settings without restarting the server. This bug has existed since Windows Server 2008 and is still present in Windows Server 2012.

In order to see the SNMP setting tab, you have to open the service settings, start the service, close the settings, and re-open the settings. This should force the tabs to appear. If this fails, try rebooting the server.

Remember to be cautious while rebooting servers or network devices during business hours.

# WMI polling issues

WMI can be more problematic than SNMP. WMI account privileges are a common WMI-related polling issue. This means that the account you are using to monitor the target server may not have adequate permission to do so. Refer to the *Creating an Active Directory service account for WMI* section of *Chapter 1, Deployment Strategy*, for procedures on how to create a privileged WMI service account, and confirm it has administrative privileges to the server you are trying to poll via WMI.

 Advanced procedures for creating an unprivileged WMI service account are referenced on the author's blog at http://justinmbrant.blogspot.com/.

# Windows firewall may be blocking WMI

This procedure will explain how to allow WMI through the Windows firewall, applicable to Windows Server 2008 R2, Windows Vista desktop operating systems, and subsequent versions.

1. Log in to a Windows OS with administrative credentials.

2. Open the **Command Prompt** by navigating to **Start | Accessories | Command Prompt**.

3. Enter the following command in the prompt:

   ```
   C:\>netsh advfirewall firewall set rule group="windows
       management instrumentation (wmi)" new enable=yes
   ```

   If **Access is denied** appears after running this command, then right-click on the **Command Prompt** shortcut and select **Run as administrator**.

 To revert this change, issue the same command but change enable=yes to enable=no.

# Windows User Account Control may be interfering with WMI

**User Account Control (UAC)** may also be a cause of WMI polling issues. As a troubleshooting step, you should disable UAC, explained in the following two referenced procedures for Windows Server 2008 R2 and Windows 7.

Be cautious while launching executable files when UAC is disabled. It is designed to protect you against malicious software.

## Steps for Windows Server 2008 R2

This procedure will explain how to disable UAC in Windows Server 2008 R2.

1. Log in to a Windows server.
2. Click on the **Start** menu and open the **Control Panel**.
3. Click on **User Accounts**.
4. In the **User Accounts** window, click on **User Accounts**.
5. Click on **Turn User Account Control on or off**.
6. Uncheck the box that says **Use User Account Control (UAC) to help protect your computer**.
7. Click on **OK** and restart the server.

 Remember to be cautious when rebooting servers or network devices during business hours.

## Steps for Windows 7

This procedure will explain how to disable UAC on Windows 7.

1. Log in to a Windows 7 machine.
2. Type UAC in the **Start** menu.
3. Click on **Change User Account Control settings**.
4. Drag the slider all the way down to **Never notify**.
5. Click on **OK** and restart the computer.

# Configuring WMI at the local computer level

This procedure explains how to manually configure WMI remote access on an individual Windows computer, as opposed to using a service account for WMI authentication.

1.  Navigate to **Start | Control Panel | Administrative Tools | Computer Management**.

2.  Expand the **Services and Applications** menu.

3.  Right-click on **WMI Control** and select **Properties**.

4.  Select the **Security** tab.

5.  Click on the **Security** button.

6.  Click on the **Add** button to add the user account. This can be a local account or domain account.

7.  Select the appropriate account and check **Remote Enable**. Click on **OK**.

# WMI Administrative Tools

If the previous troubleshooting steps did not resolve your issue, then try installing **WMI Administrative Tools**. This utility includes a WMI browser that will allow you to connect to a remote machine and browse through WMI information, which will help pinpoint the issue.

Download **WMI Administrative Tools** from Microsoft: `http://www.microsoft.com/en-us/download/details.aspx?id=24045`.

# Index

# S

 **Thank you for buying**
**SolarWinds Server & Application Monitor:**
**Deployment and Administration**

# About Packt Publishing

Packt, pronounced 'packed', published its first book "*Mastering phpMyAdmin for Effective MySQL Management*" in April 2004 and subsequently continued to specialize in publishing highly focused books on specific technologies and solutions.

Our books and publications share the experiences of your fellow IT professionals in adapting and customizing today's systems, applications, and frameworks. Our solution based books give you the knowledge and power to customize the software and technologies you're using to get the job done. Packt books are more specific and less general than the IT books you have seen in the past. Our unique business model allows us to bring you more focused information, giving you more of what you need to know, and less of what you don't.

Packt is a modern, yet unique publishing company, which focuses on producing quality, cutting-edge books for communities of developers, administrators, and newbies alike. For more information, please visit our website: www.packtpub.com.

# Writing for Packt

We welcome all inquiries from people who are interested in authoring. Book proposals should be sent to author@packtpub.com. If your book idea is still at an early stage and you would like to discuss it first before writing a formal book proposal, contact us; one of our commissioning editors will get in touch with you.

We're not just looking for published authors; if you have strong technical skills but no writing experience, our experienced editors can help you develop a writing career, or simply get some additional reward for your expertise.

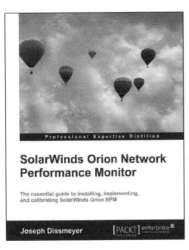

Made in the USA
Middletown, DE
12 March 2017